SHARING THE SUCCESS

Sharing the Success

THE STORY OF NFC

Peter Thompson

COLLINS
8 Grafton Street, London W1
1990

William Collins Sons & Co. Ltd
London · Glasgow · Sydney · Auckland
Toronto · Johannesburg

BRITISH LIBRARY CATALOGUING IN PUBLICATION DATA

Thompson, Peter, *1928–*
Sharing the success.
1. Great Britain.   Freight transport services:
National Freight Corporation. Denationalisation
I. Title
388.0490941

ISBN 0-00-215389-0

First published in 1990
Copyright © Peter Thompson 1990

Photoset in Linotron Meridien by
Rowland Phototypesetting Ltd,
Bury St Edmunds, Suffolk

Printed and bound in Great Britain by
William Collins Sons & Co. Ltd, Glasgow

For Lydia
Gail, Michael, Mandy, Emma and Harriet

Contents

Acknowledgements

The book is about NFC people. Their support, efforts and talents have created the success in which we all share. Many have had a direct input by reminding me of happenings which had significance or humour, and which were worth the re-telling.

Jean Adams, my secretary, worked long hours translating my almost illegible longhand into a typewritten and readable script. Irvinder Toor, one of NFC's new graduate trainees, gave up her holiday to help with the research and verification. I did not believe I had a book in me until I was persuaded so by my literary agent, Felicity Bryan. I have had great support from the Collins team led by Carol O'Brien. I thank them all.

But, above all, it was the encouragement of my wife Lydia that made sure the book was completed. She often put a glass of whisky in my hand and pushed me on to the balcony of our house in Spain, or into the study at home, with the admonition, 'It's time for you to do some more scribbling.' Without this exhortation I know my natural indolence would have taken over, and the book would not have been published.

Finally, I much appreciate the forbearance and understanding of all my family and friends who for the last year must have been bored to death as I tried out on them the stories, ideas and thoughts that have gone into the book. It isn't easy to rub shoulders with a would-be author about to give birth to his first publication. That we have emerged from the experience still friends at the end of it says much for their tolerance.

Sir Peter Thompson,
November 1989

1

The Announcement

'One of the best bits of news the government
has had for some time.'
> *Financial Times*, 19 June 1981

'This botch job dreamed up by management
and endorsed by a government which normally shows precious little sympathy for
organized labour is likely to end up in tears.'
> *Financial Guardian*, 19 June 1981

On Thursday, 18 June 1981 the same announcement was being
made in two very different places in London. In the House
of Commons at 4.13 the Right Honourable Norman Fowler,
Secretary of State for Transport in the Thatcher government,
rose to his feet. He had an important statement to make:

> A group of senior management at the National Freight
> Company have put in a £50m bid to buy the firm. The
> group plans to seek outside financial support to form a
> consortium of managers and employees to own the firm.
> The proposal is at an early stage, and there are still a lot
> of details to be worked out, but I have encouraged the
> group to press on with their plans . . . This is an imagina-
> tive and exciting proposal and I have told the managers
> concerned that I hope it will prove possible to achieve
> such a sale.

Thus was launched the concept of a unique form of employee
capitalism to the political audience.

In another location, the Accountants Hall in the City of

11

London, a very unlikely trio faced a battery of journalists and tele-vision cameras to deliver to the public and to the financial world that same message. Heading the team was a large, rather overweight, bald man who had the remnants of a Yorkshire accent. He was little known outside the world of transport. How *I* came to be in this situation is what this book is in part about.

I was supported by two smaller, younger colleagues. One was a lawyer, Philip Mayo, a man of monkish appearance, slightly hard of hearing (not a good quality in a lawyer) with an inventive mind and a waspish sense of humour. The other was an account-ant, James Watson. He had all the physical attributes of a City man, silver-haired, suave, blue-suited with a white collar over a striped shirt. He had been born in Watford and held the view that anywhere north of this fair town was a spiritual and cultural wilderness. Nonetheless – thank goodness – he understood the ways of City men.

Alongside us was a reluctant participant in the proceedings. He was our only sign of financial respectability – the man from Barclays Merchant Bank, Michael Peterson. 'Reluctant' is not an unfair description. Only that very morning a fairly heated and emotional discussion had taken place with our financial backers. They had advanced the view that while they were in total support of the employee buy-out, they were not sure that we had solved enough of the legal, political and financial problems to justify their supportive presence on this occasion. They knew more than we did about the problems ahead! But I knew they had to be there – without the presence of financial backers we had no credibility. To their eternal credit, they reversed their decision and were alongside us as we launched the concept to a typically sceptical media.

The scheme we presented was simple. We would buy the National Freight Company from the government for between £50m and £60m. We would invite all our employees and pen-sioners to buy shares in the new company being set up to purchase NFC. We estimated that the employees could raise £5m, for which they would own the vast majority of the shares. The balance of the purchase price would be lent by the banks. It looked as if we might need up to £100m in cash and credit lines.

It was at the time by far the largest buy-out that had ever been attempted in the UK. It was the *only* employee buy-out. The media questioned us closely. What would be the precise financial structure? What security would we be giving to the lending banks? Was it a cooperative we were proposing? Didn't we know that almost all the cooperatives set up by Wedgwood-Benn had failed? What made us believe that our employees would invest?

The key question was addressed to Mike Peterson. 'Why is the great Barclays supporting the scheme?' Peterson drew himself to his full height of 5'8" and walked, with measured tread, like a straining bulldog, to the microphone. He uttered but one word: 'Greed.' Effective, but hardly the foundation on which to build a great visionary concept!

William Keegan, writing in the *Guardian* the following day, saw exactly what it was all about.

> It is difficult to say whether the proposal is left wing (worker ownership of industry) or right wing in that employees are being turned into mini-capitalists. The new company being controlled by the management on a day-to-day basis will be quite different from a typical cooperative in which democracy and entrepreneurial flair often sit uneasily together. It will also be unlike the newly fashionable management buy-outs in which a small group of top managers purchase their company, since it is the intention that all employees will be involved. Although management will be in control, the directors will nevertheless have to be re-elected each year at the Company's annual meeting by the shareholders, who will in this case also be the worker/owners.

The political announcement was met with a knee-jerk reaction from Her Majesty's opposition, delivered by the Right Honourable Albert Booth, the Shadow Transport Secretary. It followed the well-worn route that the Labour Party had predetermined – they were against any privatization measure. Albert Booth made two main points. 'We are totally opposed to the sale of yet another efficient, well-managed, profitable public service,' and 'Will it be possible to sell the company at anything other than a

distress price in the present state of the road haulage market?'
The two points seemed contradictory.

Norman Fowler was quick to respond. 'The Company lost £4m
last year. To try to suggest that this is a highly profitable business
is something that no one who knew anything about the business
could accept.' It did not occur to the Labour Party that an
employee-owned company would be more in keeping with
traditional socialistic mainstream dogma than the route of
nationalization which had failed to fulfil any of the early hopes
and expectations in human and efficiency terms. The nationalized industries were sacrosanct and any change of ownership
was to be opposed.

The two major players, Norman Fowler and Albert Booth, had
crossed swords on many occasions when their roles had been
reversed in the closing months of the Callaghan Labour government. From 1975 onwards Norman Fowler, quick-witted,
well-prepared and articulate, had mercilessly criticized the
poor-performing National Freight Corporation under state ownership. He had been particularly scathing about the attempts
made in the mid-1970s to take NFC into Europe through acquisitions – all of which went sadly awry. Albert Booth, honest, and
with a slow northern delivery, had stoutly defended NFC, arguing
that service was what NFC was about, with freight integration
its secondary role.

Yet, some three years later, there was a strange reversal of
roles. Norman Fowler was encouraging NFC towards a new,
exciting future in the form of worker ownership, while Albert
Booth, the yesteryear supporter of NFC, was trying to tie its
future to the old form of ownership which had so palpably failed.

The roots of NFC went back to 1967 when Barbara Castle,
Transport Minister in the Wilson government, decided that two
things should happen to the road transport industry in the UK.
First, it would be deregulated. Up until 1968, long-distance
and commercial transport was controlled by a licensing system.
Anyone wishing to join the industry, or to start a new service,
had 'to prove' that the service was needed. These regulations
spawned a breed of lawyers 'to prove' in traffic courts that no
new entrants were ever needed. For years nothing upset the
calm waters of the Industry club. It seems strange that the

change when it did come should have been initiated by a Labour government, who were historically in favour of regulation to protect the interests of the rail lobby. In future all a new entrant was required to do was to show that he could operate safely. Deregulation was to bring competition to road haulage with a vengeance.

The second change brought about by Barbara Castle's Act was the setting up of the National Freight Corporation, merging under its wing all the road freight activities that the government had acquired over many years. BRS*, Pickfords, National Carriers (the old Sundries division of BR, which had the distinction of losing £25m on a £25m turnover in 1969, its first year of being managed by NFC), Tayforth, Harold Wood were some of the companies that came under the NFC umbrella. A spotty lot; some good – many bad – needing subsidy to survive in the early years. This was the raw material of NFC. During the passage of the 1968 Transport Act, Barbara Castle moved on to other things and Dick (now Lord) Marsh took over as Secretary of State for Transport. So it might be said Barbara Castle was the mother of NFC and Dick Marsh its midwife!

During the 1970s Sir Daniel Pettit was Chairman. A man of great personal charm and charisma, he had a very clear vision of where NFC should be taken. He was an admirable chairman. He also combined with it the role of chief executive, a difficult combination of responsibility. I myself attempted the two jobs for some three years and came to recognize the problems. The requirements of the two jobs are very different and rarely will you find the qualities in the same man to do both.

Fundamentally, the chairman's role is to make sure that the company has a long-term strategy that will ensure its success. He is also the custodian of the company's reputation with investors, customers and suppliers, and the outside world. His main concern should be for the future. The chief executive's main role is to drive the company forward on a day-to-day basis, making sure that it achieves its short-term plans. He should also be concerned about the employees and their motivation. Clearly the roles overlap. But there are two distinct jobs and in an ideal world

---

* British Road Services

they should not be combined – never mind the pressure of time involved attempting to fulfil both roles.

The vision was clear: NFC had to get into more sophisticated services (over 75 per cent of the turnover in 1968 was in parcels and general haulage where we would have no real natural advantage over small competitors once deregulation allowed them to enter the market and compete). We had to internationalize and start earning profits in Europe. We had to become more efficient, particularly in the use of labour. We had to find a way of working with the powerful trade unions, in particular the Transport & General Workers' Union and the National Union of Railwaymen. This would not be easy, as they were – and still are – unwilling to work with each other.

Progress was made in the early 1970s and the need for subsidy disappeared in 1973. A mass assault was launched to make NFC as big in Europe as it was in the UK by the end of the decade. This was principally to be accomplished by acquisitions in France, Belgium, Holland and Germany. But with the oil-induced recession of 1975/76, NFC's recovery was not strong enough. It slumped back into losses which, after interest, amounted to £31m. The principal problem was the European acquisitions which were rightly criticized by Norman Fowler. Their selection had not been good; subsequently they became massive loss makers. They had to be closed at no small cost to the tax payer.

In the late 1970s the fortunes of NFC improved, and by 1980 it seemed to the Conservative government that progress had been sufficient to justify preparing the company for flotation on the London Stock Exchange. We were turned by Act of Parliament into a limited liability company. The balance sheet was reconstructed. We were all dressed up and ready to go when disaster struck like twin-forked lightning.

The first fork was the deep recession that hit the whole Western world in 1979/80 but which was particularly severe in the UK. In the space of twelve months manufacturing output dropped by some 15 per cent. As we were principally serving manufacturing industry, some 15 per cent of our customers disappeared almost overnight. It was in many ways a much more severe recession than the UK experienced in the 1930s. Consequently our profitability declined and we slipped into losses again.

The second fork was a government own goal. The very day in June 1980 that the Queen signed and hence enacted the 1980 Transport Act which prepared NFC for privatization, Norman Fowler had a discussion with Sir Peter Parker, Chairman of British Rail. Efficiency and profit improvement were the subjects on the agenda. One of the many loss-making services which BR operated was an express parcels service (BREPS). It was losing, so it was rumoured, £1 for every £1 of revenue (reminiscent of National Carriers when it came out of the Railways in 1968). Parker sought agreement to close the service but required the government to fund the redundancy costs. Norman Fowler agreed that this would be money well spent.

What has this to do with NFC? Historically NFC had provided on long-term contract the 2400 vehicles and 2800 men to carry out the collection and delivery operations of the service which BR managed, operated and marketed. The contract was worth £25m a year to NFC, and it was profitable. It was by far our largest contract, representing some 7 per cent of our turnover.

It was hardly surprising, against a background of recession, falling profits and loss of *the* major profitable contract, that Schroder Wragg, the merchant bank advising the government, concluded that the City would be unlikely to invest in the company until something improved! Their message to the government was, 'Phone us in two years' time if NFC manages itself out of the problems that it has, and meets the ambitious profit-improvement targets it has set itself.'

It was with this background that the three unlikely lads, clutching to them their merchant banker, were attempting to launch the impossibly difficult concept of an employee buy-out. A management buy-out would have been difficult enough. Why complicate it by involving the employees? The answer lay in the background of the key players, but in particular in my own beliefs which had been moulded over fifty years.

2

Setting the Values

'Give me a child until he is seven and he
will be ours for life.'   JESUIT PROVERB

'Religions change: beer and wine remain.'
HERVEY ALLEN & ANTHONY ADVERSE

I owe my early moulding to my mother, coupled with a Yorkshire
upbringing. Although having just claimed a Yorkshire breeding,
I must confess that I was actually born in Northumberland.
It happened in a small seaside resort called Monkseaton near
Tyneside. My parents had temporarily left 'the broad acres' to
earn a living further north. My father owned and ran a men's
outfitting shop in Newcastle. The business was a victim of the
recession and he had to put it into liquidation. In 1928, the year
of my birth, we removed to the other end of the country, to
Kent. My father had applied for, and obtained, the managership
of Burton, the tailor's shop in Margate. We were a happy united
family – father, mother, and three boys all under the age of
seven.

Within two years my father had had a severe cerebral stroke
which affected his speech and reduced his mental capacity. His
illness meant that we had to return to Bradford in Yorkshire to
live with my grandmother, and she helped to look after us while
my mother went to work.

In her younger days my mother had been a successful
fashionwear saleswoman. She worked with one or more of the
great couturier houses. The highlight of her year was to spend
time at Windsor Castle during Ascot week, fitting and arranging

dresses for members of the Royal party. To support us she decided to seek a job with the local department store as a saleswoman in their fur department. A far cry from the salons of Bond Street. We were not conscious of any deprivation as children. But when I think back on how difficult it must have been for her to look after an invalid husband, three boisterous young boys, to hold down a full-time job and to contend with constant financial problems, I cannot but admire her stamina and her love for us all which kept her going.

There were many ways in which she moulded us. Even today some of the advice she used to give still encroaches into my business life. 'Do what's right and shame the devil,' she used to say. How often this has been the guiding principle in taking a difficult decision when it might have been more profitable in the short term to have been expedient and have fudged the issue.

I remember as a small boy stealing apples with my brother from the outside display of the local greengrocer. Brian stole the apples – I kept watch. My mother found us out and made us report our misdemeanour to the local police station. We then had to go to the greengrocer, apologize and pay for the apples, which meant no spending money for two weeks.

We purchased a company in NFC and found that the management was passing discounts in cash to individuals who gave them business. Some 60 per cent of their business was done this way. When I found out my reaction was unequivocal – I gave the management three months to stop the practice despite the advice that it could well mean we lost most of the business. In fact, we lost little, but it was a risk. However, with my mother's precepts clearly imprinted on my mind, I had had no doubt about what should be done.

'There's nowt for hard lines' – 'nothing for bad luck' – has become part of NFC's philosophy. How often when a company is doing well does the top management team claim the credit for it? Their brilliant reading of the market place, or their exceptional operational skills, caused it all. However, when profits fall, economic recession and depressed demand are to blame. It is nothing at all to do with a lack of management skill. Yet good managers somehow seem to be able to push their business ahead regardless of external factors. Witness Sir Owen Green, arguably the best

UK manager of the last twenty years, who has increased BTR's*
profits and earnings per share every year since 1972 when he
took over the company, despite three major economic recessions.
If you believe in personal accountability, as we do in NFC, there
can be 'nowt for hard lines'.

Despite having to look after an invalid husband until he died
aged 79, losing my two brothers, one killed in the war, the other
dying from Hodgkin's disease aged 27, my mother has remained
to this day, at the age of 96, forceful, alert, critical of me when
it is deserved, and has retained a forward-looking optimistic
approach to life. Truly a great lady and a great fighter.

She recognized that she needed help with our education,
so she applied for places for my elder brother and me at The
Warehousemen, Clerks & Drapers Schools. These two boarding
schools, one for boys and one for girls, supported principally by
the retail drapery trade, were for children of employees who had
fallen on hard times. Today, like many schools which started
as charitable establishments, it is now a thriving, fee-paying,
coeducational boarding school called the Royal Russell School.

So I went away to school at the age of seven, and, apart from
spending the first night back at school after each holiday crying
myself to sleep (this went on, I am ashamed to say, until I
was fourteen!), I enjoyed and benefited enormously from the
education. I revelled in games – cricket, soccer and hockey, and
had little difficulty in representing the school at every age group
in all three. I found that I had an ability to do better in exams
than the work I did during the term merited.

You may think life is unfair in this respect. How many people
are diligent and well-prepared, and yet blow it when they come
to the true test? I seem to be the opposite. For example, in
normal conversation I tend to stutter and frequently search
unsuccessfully for the right word. On my feet, before an audience, under stress all this hesitation disappears. Success, therefore, is all about performance on the day. The emphasis in
modern education on continuous assessment is about fairness,
but business success is regrettably not about fairness but about

* Birmingham Tyre & Rubber Company

achievement. I am sure most football managers would share my view.

One side of school life I did not enjoy was the Cadet Corps. I lack the kind of discipline required to make a successful military man. Before making any decision, I always want to examine and debate all the possible alternatives. This is not the way that armies win wars. If a battle is to be won, every man must know precisely what he has to do, and be prepared to carry out orders without question. A democratic and participative management style in war just would not work.

A lifelong friend of mine at school was Angus McGill who today is a journalist and writes a weekly column in the *Evening Standard*. He too was not a military man. Unfortunately, however, he was a barrack room lawyer. He read the school rules which stated that membership of the Cadet Corps was voluntary. Within living memory no-one at the school had ever *not* been in the Corps. We decided to resign. After much legal disputation our right to resign was established and we left the Corps. You can imagine the disgrace of it all, since all this was going on whilst outside the premises a world war to save civilization was being waged. Our revolt against the establishment was not long-lived. Every Tuesday and Thursday the conchies (us conscientious objectors were so designated) were required to parade elsewhere from the cadets and spend the afternoon in physically-punishing activity – like digging the school garden. Alas at this age I was not prepared to suffer too much for my principles so we rejoined the Cadets. I was not the stuff of which martyrs are made!

It was rather early in life that I began to develop a political awareness. I felt that things in society were not just and that change was needed. My first reaction, being a fundamentalist, was to embrace anarchy. After all, why did we need government? Wouldn't the world be a better place without restrictive laws and politicians? Man was basically good, and it was only power-seeking politicians who prevented mankind living in harmony without government. This was my earliest political testimony.

I carried my beliefs a little too far when, in a fit of exuberance with five other prefects (by this time I had begun to acquire 'power' myself), we raised the symbol of revolt – a chamber pot – to the top of the school flagpole. This act was accompanied by much rhetoric. The flagpole was on top of a hill that could be seen by most of the inhabitants of the neighbouring town of Croydon. The revolutionary symbol was fine at night when it was raised – it was less acceptable when we couldn't get it down, and there it stayed until morning. We had no alternative other than to confess to the headmaster, who administered the appropriate punishment.

It wasn't too long, therefore, before anarchy receded as a political concept. Another ideology took over. I had moved on to take my higher school certificate at Bradford Grammar School. This northern grammar school to this day is one of the finest schools in the land. Regularly it turns out more than its share of Oxbridge and other university entrants, sportsmen and top-rate businessmen. Here I fell under the influence of a very compelling history and economics master, Gus Shepherd. He opened my mind to the historical and economic truth of the Marxist labour theory of value. I was captivated to the point where I rationalized all history in terms of economic phenomena. Later, seeking an entry to Sidney Sussex College, Cambridge, I explained to the examiners that Henry VIII was simply a capitalist exploiting the working classes. Needless to say, my application was rejected! However, the socialist views that I embraced at this early stage stayed with me for a long time.

I was still at school when the war in Europe finished. A general election was called. To the absolute horror of my family I attended the massive Conservative open-air election rally in the centre of Bradford at which Winston Churchill spoke. I joined in the heckling – although on reflection he didn't seem to have too much trouble dealing with our ritualistic chants. It was my only chance, not yet having the vote, to demand political changes. I was excited, as were many young people, particularly those returning from the war, when the Labour government was elected. Reform was in the air.

The almost religious banner of true socialism would be raised in England's fair and pleasant land. 'From each according to his ability, to each according to his need' would be the principles which would govern our country. The means of production would be nationalized and everyone would work better, and with more purpose, because they would be motivated by service to the community rather than by self-interest. Industrial relations would be transformed, and the 'us and them' attitude between management and workers would disappear as we all worked for a common purpose. These were the ideals on which the Labour government was elected, and they appealed to me at the age of seventeen. The process of disillusionment was slow and was not complete until I had worked in two nationalized industries and found that the reality was far from the theory.

After leaving school at the age of eighteen, I went off to do my National Service. I was a less than enthusiastic soldier. The war was over, the purpose of conscription seemed obscure, and it was preventing me from getting on with my real life. The two and a half years passed slowly, but it did give me some insights into what a sheltered life I had led to date.

For some obscure reason, two of the more worldly troopers in the Royal Armoured Corps unit at Bovington 'adopted' me. I was a curly headed, fresh-faced youngster straight out of school. These two, at the same age as me, were mature and seasoned men. They had both gone into the steelworks at the age of fifteen, had been drinking beer in the working men's club from the same age, and had been sampling the joys of feminine company from an even earlier age. They took me like a mascot under their wing. They showed me another side of life. It was their idea of a great night out to drink at least ten pints of beer, to pick a fight with anyone in sight, and finish the night in the arms of any willing and amenable local lass they could find. I took to these new pursuits with the enthusiasm of a convert who has just found religion. These years in the army certainly developed the earthy side of my character and even to this day I am as content in the company of men who work with their hands as with men who work with their minds.

I left the army having reached the rank of Corporal and went straight to university. I was happy enough to go to Leeds, where after a year majoring in history I transferred to an economics degree course. This coincided with the decision I took *not* to become a teacher. I had believed this would be my calling until I actually tried it.

I turned up at Middleton Road Junior School in Bradford to do my first teaching practice. The school was right in the heart of one of the tougher areas of the city. It attracted more than its share of seven- and eight-year-old hooligans. The headmaster, a gentle, kind and sensitive man who saw only good in his pupils, denied to his teaching staff the use of the well-directed cuff over the ear or indeed the judicial administration of the cane. Consequently, keeping any semblance of order in the classroom, particularly by a student teacher unable to make use of the best weapon in his inadequate armoury, was impossible. I came away a chastened and defeated would-be educator of the young.

My mind turned to other ways of earning a living and industry seemed to beckon. I dropped history and took up economics, which seemed to be more relevant to my future. I need not have bothered. The other graduates taken on by my first employer had read classics, social science and ancient history . . .

I loved university – the environment of acquiring knowledge, the cut and thrust of political debate, the freedom of choosing how to spend one's time, the endless hours of drinking, gossiping and playing bridge. It should be a part of everyone's education. I believe debate to be the life-blood of innovation. Many are the hours I spent deliberately taking the opposite view to that being advanced, not because I necessarily believed it, but because in this way the proposition is examined in depth.

In NFC our style is one of open debate. I always look for the unconventional, the different approach, the thinking of the unthinkable, and do not take any advice, whether legal, corporate or accountancy, without challenging it. At times our board meetings, and indeed other meetings, become heated because the process of challenge to conventional wisdom is frustrating to the individual being challenged. At the same time, it is the one way of ensuring that the company does not become conventional. Conventionality is mediocrity. No market leader can afford to be consistently conventional. I have held these views, which were formed in the Students' Union and bedsits of Leeds University, and indeed around the firesides of the gang of friends I had in Bradford, most of my adult life.

24

From all the economic theory and analysis that I was exposed to while studying for my degree, one concept in particular, which embraces a practical reality, lodged in my mind. It is the concept of 'opportunity cost'. For example, if we wanted to acquire a new company in the US, we would be unable to afford to expand as many depots in the UK – the scarcest resource usually being not money but good management. The cost of doing something is really the lost opportunity of doing something else.

Most forceful managements I have worked with mistakenly believe they can do everything, and it is often as a result of overlooking this 'opportunity cost' that they make the wrong decision. The cost of doing anything must always include the cost of the opportunity which has been lost of doing something else.

It was time to get a job. In my last term of university the milk round that takes place today was at its embryonic stage. Companies needing to recruit graduates send teams of managers to the universities to extol the virtues of their company, and to try to persuade the better graduates to join their firm. Today the competition is killing, with dozens of applications for every place, but in 1952 graduates were in relatively short supply. At the time, Unilever was one of the most sought-after graduate traineeships for many reasons. First, they had developed a reputation for training people to be good managers, rather than using graduates as over-educated salesmen and clerks, as did many other companies. Unilever had sorted out a thorough selection process. Above all, they were an international company, clearly in the forefront of satisfying the boom for consumer products that was being unleashed throughout the world in the aftermath of the rationing and shortages of the war period. With little hope of being selected, I applied for a traineeship with Unilever.

I well remember turning up at Unilever House for a one and a half day contest. About twenty of us were being assessed. We knew only two or three would be chosen. To be chosen you obviously had to impress the team of Unilever senior managers who were the selectors. But it was also necessary to try to win the vote of the other members of the group. In the final interview each candidate was asked, 'If you are not elected yourself, to which of the other candidates would you offer the job?' Much attention was paid to this, as it is clearly important for a potential manager to be able to command the support of his peer group.

The first step was to introduce yourself to the group. As I listened to the background of the others – many of them with honours degrees from Oxbridge, officers returning from the forces having reached field rank and with a proven history of command, some with accountancy or legal qualifications – my first reaction was one of deep pessimism. What chance had I? A graduate from a redbrick university, with a pronounced York-shire accent, and a dismal military career. These were the qualifi-cations and experience I was offering.

In that day and a half of close assessment, I learnt some early lessons about group leadership. First, don't start talking too early, the early star is unlikely to stay the pace. Secondly, wait for the guy to emerge whom no one in the group can stand – there will always be one who is too arrogant, too condescending, too opinionated who everyone else detests. Try to be prominent in the counterattack against this type of individual. This will demonstrate to the others that you are able to assess an individ-ual's character. There will always be somebody who, on the surface, has all the charisma – is good-looking, articulate and full of common sense. The rest of the group will recognize him and know he is the one they each have to beat. Don't ally yourself to him, otherwise the group will attack the alliance. Above all, recognize that stamina is critical and probably what the observers are seeking above everything. They know, as all managers know, that stamina and effectiveness are close neighbours. Have you noticed how very often it is the persistent guy who gets the girl, and vice versa?

So, after one and a half days of interviews, group discussions and debate, I was still in there pitching. Dripping away, as my friends would say. I am convinced that it was this more than anything else that caused Unilever to offer me one of their prized central management traineeships.

What then followed was pure farce. That year, 1952, was, I believe, the first year that Unilever had centrally recruited all its management trainees. After the selection process it was then necessary for a subsidiary company formally to employ the trainee and to guide his early career. I was selected to go to the Walls ice cream and meat company, and I had a highly satisfactory interview with two of the directors – the Chairman of the company being overseas at the time. I was offered, and I accepted, a traineeship with them. I started with enthusiasm one Monday morning in September, proud to have my first job. Within two hours I was sent for by the now-returned Chairman.

He asked me but three questions. 'Are you prepared to work anywhere in the UK or indeed in the world for my company?'

'Yes, sir, anywhere. Even Wigan,' I replied.

'Are you prepared to work long hours for the company?'

'Yes, sir, twenty-four hours a day if need be.'

'Are you married, or have you any attachments which would distract you from working effectively in the company?'

'No, sir, I am not married. I have no regular girlfriends, and if needs be I can live out of a suitcase.' I mentally registered one hundred per cent.

He paused a minute and then said, 'Clearly, young man, you are not of the quality that Walls need in their management trainees. You have no job here. You had better go back from whence you came!' I could only presume he was looking for static, married, nine-to-five men.

I was shattered! I had been fired within two hours of starting my business life. Years later I was told it was a political decision, that the Chairman wouldn't put up with Unilever House telling him which trainees to employ.

I spent a month at home while Unilever found another slot for me. Fortunately, it was to be as a specialist trainee in transport management. My career was by chance set in the direction that it has followed ever since. Who says luck is not important?

Two years of training followed, which in some ways were excellent. During the two years I was exposed to many aspects of Unilever's transport, shipping and warehousing activities. I also spent nine months with the major providers of transport in the UK: British Rail, the Port of London Authority and the Road Haulage Executive whose main company was BRS. It is ironic

27

that the main transport company of Unilever was SPD* which, much later, along with BRS, was to become part of NFC. The scope of the training was wide and comprehensive but it was training by observation. Throughout the whole of my two years there, I actually organized and managed nothing except myself. It was rubber-necking for too long. Modern graduate training demands much more practical and hands-on experience to be given to the young manager.

So at last, at the age of twenty-seven I started my management career. I was almost trained to indolence; I needed some action. I was posted to be assistant transport manager at Unilever's major soap works in Warrington. I spent one year helping on the transport side and another on the warehousing. It was a marvellous place to begin one's management life. First of all, there were so many different aspects of transport on which to try my hand. We still had a few horses, a transporter bridge, pipelines, barges sailing up and down the ship canal, trucks, tankers and a comprehensive railway system. It was a veritable Aladdin's cave for the transport enthusiast. For years the works had been used for developing young managers, and there was a good number of us there.

We were licked into shape by the long-serving departmental managers to whom we reported, and also by the long-suffering foremen who were the backbone of the business. Rather in the way sergeant-majors treat young officers in the army, so the foremen made it clear that they were really in charge but at the same time took pride in the development of the young managers who they helped on their way.

One of the awesome responsibilities I had in the warehouse was to try and keep separate, on Christmas Eve, the nubile young ladies who packed Persil into containers on the first floor of the Persil building, from the teenage lads who loaded the containers into the railway trucks on the ground floor. I felt like Horatio defending the bridge as I stood on the staircase between the floors. The plant prided itself on keeping production going until the normal closing time on Christmas Eve. The Chairman ordained that it should be so. His was not the task of trying to curb

* Originally known by the ghastly name of Speedy Prompt Delivery

the natural instincts of the young who had enjoyed a Christmas drink together during the lunch break. I learnt one good management lesson, which was that it is no good ordaining from on high the impossible. Needless to say, my bridgehead was swept aside when attacked from both sides with the girls trying to get down and the boys trying to get up . . .

I also learned a little about individual appraisal – so important in my business philosophy that it will come up time and again. When I was given responsibility, albeit temporarily, for a particular transport section, I was told that one of the drivers was a hopeless, idle malingerer, filthy of appearance and frequently rude to customers. I called him in after I had observed him for a couple of days. I said, 'George, you are awful. Everything you do is terrible,' and I went on to list his failures as a worker and as a human being. As he left, he turned and said, 'Thank you, gov.'

'But,' I said, 'all I told you was that you were awful.'

'Well,' said George, 'at least that shows you care.'

This early experience taught me that people do want their boss to appraise them. If this is not done, how can anyone improve? There is nothing so unacceptable to an individual as his boss's indifference. I have been a believer in appraisals ever since. Eventually George did, marginally, improve, but regrettably not enough. I can only think the appraisal was fine, but the follow-up training was not a success. (Mind you, with George it would have taken a miracle!)

They were two happy years in Warrington and during that time I made one of the best decisions in my life, which was to marry a local farmer's daughter, Patricia. She was ten years younger than me. I suppose at the age of nineteen she could hardly have known what she was taking on. It is quite true that, if he is to succeed, a man needs a loving supportive wife to create the stable base from which the twentieth-century business warrior goes forth to battle, and this she did to perfection.

My future lay in the honeyed south. I came to London to join a small but fast-developing frozen food company called Birds Eye Foods, part of the mighty Unilever empire. My northern upbringing provided me, I believe, with a number of strengths that have stood me in good stead over the years. Yorkshire folk have little regard for vanity. For example, if an attractive girl goes into a room with a spot on the end of her nose which she has used all the cosmetic skills in her power to disguise, the opening remark may well be, 'Ee, our Betty, that's a terrible boil you've got on the end of your nose.' Similarly, I remember buying my first suit and wearing it to a party given by one of my friends whose father was a mill owner. I thought I looked immensely smart. He greeted me warmly, shook my hand, felt the lapel of the new suit. 'Very smart, not a bad bit of Batley,' he announced to the assembled guests. Batley, as all woolmen know, is the town famed for manufacturing horse blankets. In that kind of society there is little chance of getting any personal achievements out of perspective.

Years later, as the Chairman of Community Hospitals, a private hospital group, I went up to Bradford to see the directors of the local private hospital in which we had a major shareholding. There had been difficulties and I had come with an olive branch in my hands to see if they could be sorted out. The local chairman opened the meeting with the usual pleasantries, by thanking me for coming and, as a busy man, for giving up time to be there. Hardly were the words out of his mouth when one of his directors interjected, 'We're having none of that – we're all bloody busy men!' I knew I was back in Yorkshire! Certainly, a Yorkshire upbringing does not allow you to become puffed-up with your own importance. It is also a strangely classless society. Perhaps this has something to do with the accent – there is no stigma attached to not speaking 'educated' or 'upper-class' English. In fact anyone affecting such an accent would be regarded as a 'fancy bugger'.

Humour is never far from the surface. The humour can be basic, cruel perhaps, but nearly always close to reality: like the woolman at the marriage of his plain daughter saying to his lifelong friend, 'This is a happy day for me. You know, I was always afraid that she would die wondering' . . .

Yorkshire also tends to give to its sons a well-developed sense of value. It is not bad form to ask the price of anything and to debate it at length – it is not by chance that Bradford is one of the cheapest places to live in the UK. I myself still shudder when a customer asks to be taken to an expensive restaurant in the certain knowledge that the bill will be astronomical. Can the small nuances of fashion and taste really be worth the premium? It is one of the reasons why NFC is not (and I suspect never will be) a company with a lavish lifestyle. No Rolls Royces, yachts or private planes – but plenty of trucks!

So much for reflections on a northern upbringing. From now on I would be earning my living in and around London. Birds Eye Foods was a wonderfully young company in the 1950s. We were the market leaders in a section of the food market which was growing exponentially. Convenience foods were demanded by the increasing number of families with two breadwinners. Each year Birds Eye was doubling its turnover, increasing its production facilities, opening new cold stores and developing more and more sophisticated methods of freezing foods and transporting it to the shops. We were a young management, arrogant about our abilities to beat the competition and led by a colossus of a man, James Parrett. It was here that for the first time in my life I began to realize what leadership was about. He had the physical attributes which enhance leadership, being over six foot tall, rugged and handsome. He was articulate and had the natural aggression of an ex-marine. He had a marketing background and it was fascinating to see him make decisions and set targets which ensured Birds Eye's market leadership.

In convenience foods the mission was to find a prepared food as universally acceptable as the sausage. The fish finger came close. But in the mid-fifties it was too expensive. Parrett recognized this, and saw the breakthrough in price terms. 'We must reduce the price from 3/6d to 2/6d for a packet of twelve. It should be a one-coin purchase.'

'Impossible,' cried the accountants.

If we could double the sales, would it then work?

'Preposterous,' said the bean counters.

But if sales were doubled, then profits could be won.

'Do it,' said Parrett, 'and what's more, spend an extra £¼m on advertising.'

Sure enough, the psychological barrier was broken. Sales more

31

than doubled. Families could afford the fish finger and to this day it is still the busy mother's equivalent of the sausage.

He must have been a reasonably tolerant man. In 1958 Birds Eye had grown to sufficient size that, under the Unilever car policy, Parrett was able to exchange his Riley for a Jaguar. He enjoyed motoring, and I, as transport manager, had pulled out all the stops to get a quick delivery of his new Jaguar. He was due to fly down in a private plane from the north to an airport in Hertfordshire called Bovingdon, close to my own home. I decided to drive the new Jaguar to the airport so that he could have it as soon as possible. Driving down a narrow country lane I encountered a large American Chevrolet – there was just not enough room to pass. I heard an awful crunch, and the side of the Jaguar was mortally wounded. I was amazed at his restraint when I met him off the plane and told him that I had managed to dent severely his new pride and joy before he had even seen it, let alone driven it. I suppose it is a sign of his leadership qualities that this was not an early end to my life in transport!

He was an exciting man to work for and he could have led all of us over any cliff he chose. Strangely enough, and this applies to many managers who are good in every other respect, he was excellent with his own team but not good with his superiors in Unilever House. It is ironic that such a talented man did not achieve the accolade of Unilever board membership, perhaps because of this weakness.

Although Birds Eye was a great company to be employed by, my own boss, who was the Commercial Director and whose reputation was founded upon an ability to cut costs, failed to recognize that job excitement is not everything. In particular, it is not everything to a man who by this time had not only a wife but three children to support. For two successive years when it came to my salary review, I claimed, and I needed, and I felt I was worth, another £200 a year. Instead of the increase I was given a lecture on thrift. I was invited to keep a record of my expenditure and my boss would show me how I could cut my cloth to match my income. If he had only given me the extra £200 per annum, I know I would still have been with Birds Eye today. But I had to leave, not because of lack of job satisfaction but just to get more money. For the last time in my life I scoured the columns of the *Daily Telegraph* and saw an advert for a transport job with the large steel and engineering company GKN.* With reluctance, after ten happy years, I left Unilever for an extra £1000 a year. The lessons I learned from this period of my business life were twofold: firstly, you can feel the power of good leadership, and, secondly, man does not live by job satisfaction alone – he does need to be reasonably paid for a job well done.

The two years I spent with GKN were an unfortunate mistake. One part of the board thought that cost savings and general improvements could best be achieved from rationalizing the distribution activities of the group. They decided to set up a central transport and shipping department to do this. The other, and more powerful faction of the board, decided that such a large and diverse business would be better motivated if more autonomy was given to the individual businesses.

I and my team identified the many large savings which could have been made if companies within the Group had cooperated and pooled resources; for example, by putting together the distribution networks of the Screws and Fasteners division with the Bolts division who were producing similar commodities and delivering them to similar customers. The savings were not made because the concept perished on the altar of divisional autonomy.

Realizing that I was trying to push water uphill by seeking inter-group cooperation, we turned ourselves into a consultancy department offering advice to various parts of the business on how they could reduce their distribution costs. One suggestion was to make better use of vehicles by making sure they were loaded on both the outward and return journeys. We worked out some interesting load combinations, like steel rods from Cardiff to Manchester being backloaded with foundry sand from Cheshire to south Wales. It meant the design of special, long-wheelbased tippers, but it saved many thousands of pounds a year. This was consultancy work, however, and I knew at heart I was a manager. I wanted to make things happen not just advise people how to save costs.

* Guest, Keen and Nettlefold

I was number two in the GKN transport hierarchy when, out of the blue, an old friend from Bradford Grammar School phoned me. He said that the Rank Organization had decided to set up a central transport operation, and asked if I was interested in running it. So, for the first time, I decided to take the top job in transport and distribution in a major company.

From my short spell with GKN I learnt never to join the centralized team of a business that was busy decentralizing, and that, for me at least, doing is better than advising. I would never again seek to be a consultant.

Soap, food, engineering, and now entertainment! The Rank Organization in the 1960s was a pot pourri of many unconnected businesses. Its core was the film-making interests of Lord Rank, originally of the flour-milling family but better known as J. Arthur Rank, whose studios at Pinewood and Denham were the core of British postwar film industry. He appointed a restless, energetic, hard and driving man to develop these interests in the late fifties. John Davis – later Sir John – was a constant source of media attention both through his business activities and his marital problems. His divorce from one of the original Rank starlets was the first under the new marriage act whereby the wife for the first time could claim capital and not just maintenance from the husband. Needless to say the divorce caused much interest as it was a test case to see to what extent the court would use its new powers and how much it would cost the errant husband.

As a businessman he had widened the horizons of the Rank Organization, and, to his great credit after many other industrialists had turned it down, he recognized the potential of the Xerox technology. He acquired the rights to market the process in the UK, Europe and a number of the overseas territories. It was so successful that it came totally to dominate the profits of the organization. His subsequent attempts to widen the group's interests into the full range of leisure activities like hotels, ten-pin bowling and holiday camps, were less successful. Whether he was a one-product man, i.e. Xerox, as some critics would say, or the man who laid the foundations for the more successful and broader-based group that it has since become will always be debated.

His management style was possibly the most authoritarian and autocratic in British industry at the time. If people did not perform, and perform quickly, they were fired. Compensation for loss of office was always very generous, but believing that the axe would descend as surely as night follows day, at the peak of this management culture people actually worked for the pay-off. This, the ultimate approach to personal accountability, went hand in hand with management by detail. John Davis had three or four secretaries who were kept busy with memos on the minutiae of each business in the organization. His chief executives were bombarded with instructions and advice. As long as the chairman is competent and his judgement is sound, this style of management can work. Indeed the Rank Organization was driven along for many years by the irrepressible energy of Sir John. But of course it did not breed management loyalty. How could it when the top executives came and went so frequently? It did not inspire and develop good people.

I left after two years because I was offered a more challenging job in a newly nationalized industry, where I would be able to see whether my early beliefs about the motivation provided by public ownership had any practical reality. The turnover of senior management was such that when I resigned with two years' service, I was the longest-serving senior executive reporting to Sir John, with the exception of his deputy chairman, Graham Dawson.

J. D. was a man we feared. At the same time he was admired for his drive, but, above all, he was a man who, once you had worked for him, you never forgot. A club was founded by people who had been sacked by him, many of whom subsequently had successful careers in British industry. It was known as the 'Rank Outsiders'. J. D. was even asked to attend the dinners, which I understand he did with some enthusiasm.

I decided from those two far-from-dull years that the Rank Organization management style would not be the one that I would adopt if I ever became a business leader. It convinced me that staff participation and involvement would be a better way of managing a business. I also felt sure that this would be the best way to develop good management. At the same time, Sir

John's style could not be dismissed as being ineffective or unsuccessful. Through his vision of Xerography he did much to enhance the wealth of his shareholders.

It was now time to leave the private sector where I had experienced at first hand many management styles. I had seen capitalism working effectively, but I was still not convinced that it was the best way of achieving profits while at the same time satisfying the aspirations of employees, who I believed would be better fulfilled helping to create wealth within industries that were owned by the nation. I also thought the public sector would provide a different management challenge, since the problems that this sector had to solve were probably the most complex and important in British industry. I looked forward to a nationalized industry proving to be a better environment for owners, management and workers to work in harmony, as they would – or should – have identical objectives.

3

Nationalization – the Years of Disillusionment

'If everybody owns something, nobody owns it. It is when something is yours that you care for it, nurture it, work to make it thrive and grow.'
JOHN MOORE, Secretary of State
for Transport

In the latter days of 1966 the Iron & Steel Nationalization Bill was being guided through parliament by the Secretary of State for Energy, the Right Honourable Richard Marsh. I was appointed head of the Transport & Shipping operations of the newly emerging British Steel. That year saw the second attempt to nationalize British Steel, the first attempt being reversed by the incoming Conservative Party in 1955 before it could be implemented. As with all nationalizations, it created a huge managerial challenge. It meant the takeover and integration of the fourteen major steel makers in the UK. It required the setting up of a management and financial structure which would enable the future rationalization of the industry. Above all, it needed a vision of the future which would unite management and workers to give them a sense of belonging to an enterprise that had challenge, inspiration and a sense of purpose.

To formulate such a vision, and to drive it into practice, British Steel needed a leader of great intellect, charisma and communication skills. He had to unite towards a common purpose all the proud private companies who were to form the new industry; and who, given a free choice, did not want to be united. In fact, they had all campaigned hard against the proposed nationalization.

This stance was somewhat hypocritical, as for many years, indeed ever since the war, all the major investment decisions in the industry had been agreed by, and, in the main, financed by, government. There was also a government-approved Federation of the industry which controlled most of the pricing, marketing and purchasing activities. Having accepted over the years this level of government intervention and market manipulation, it really should not have been such a steep hill to climb to accept state ownership and management.

It would have been better if the future leader of British Steel could have been found from within the industry, but, because of their vocal opposition to nationalization, the natural leaders in the industry virtually disqualified themselves. It is always a problem for a Labour government to find top businessmen to carry out the monumental management tasks that nationalization demands. After a protracted search the choice fell on the relatively youthful Lord Melchett. His background was in merchant banking, and, whilst his grandfather had been an industrial colossus forging by takeover and merger the great ICI, Julian Melchett had no such experience of industry, restructuring or rationalizing. His early death long before the task was complete was a tragedy, as he was an able, popular and good man.

From the beginning, in order to obtain some level of co-operation from the barons of the industry, Melchett had to compromise. When BSC was first formed, the organization was initially based upon the old company loyalties. This clearly could not last, as the old company structure had no logic once ownership had changed. It did not make sense to have the basic iron and strip steel production in separate groups. In the four years I was there, there were to be two more reorganizations; the first production based, the next partially market based.

Reorganization is not a good thing for any business. At times it is obviously necessary, but in deciding on a particular organization, the aim should be that it remains relevant for at least five years – and preferably longer. Not one of the reorganizations that I witnessed in BSC had the chance of meeting this criterion. They were expedient compromises made with a view to placating particular vested interests. Any reorganization is disruptive. It makes key management take their eye off the only ball that should ever be in play – the satisfaction of the customer. It produces in-plays in which each individual seeks to find for himself a role and to ensure that when the new cards are dealt, he gets the hand he wants. It is also usually accompanied by an examination of the level of delegation that can be given to each new layer of management, and only rarely does this actually lead to an increase in the level of local autonomy. In the three attempts at settling the long-term organization that I witnessed in British Steel, there was never any increase in the level of local autonomy.

I am not a great reader of books on management theory. I prefer to read the biographies of businessmen who have performed and from them draw my own management lessons. An early hero of mine was Robert Townsend, who revitalized the Avis company and who wrote a good account of it in a book called *Up the Organization*. One of the central themes of his business practice was to allow more freedom to operating companies, to get rid of central departments and their associated costs. As I sat in the centre of the new British Steel, it was like a nightmare reversal of all the precepts which he had so amusingly preached.

In short order, the executive jets started to arrive; millions were spent on revamping the London headquarters to standards of luxury unbecoming to a hardly profitable business; the public relations and advertising departments were afforded priority status – countless millions were spent upon trying to increase the use of steel through television and media advertising, a campaign more appropriate to a consumer product than a base material. Furthermore, the political and corporate strategists assembled in sizeable numbers, and a large personnel department headed by a recruit from the Trade Union movement was an early priority. It was hardly surprising that from being a profitable business at the time of nationalization, British Steel became hugely unprofitable and a constant drain on the public purse throughout the 1970s, at one time losing more than £1m per day.

It was a time of seeming euphoria. Countless working parties were formed to plan the expansion of existing capacity and the development of green field sites to satisfy the ever-increasing estimates of the demand for steel worldwide. All these grandiose plans were to founder as the worldwide demand for steel collapsed in the wake of the successive oil crises in the 1970s.

Growth-based corporate plans were presented to government – the banker – and argued over interminably, while smaller, more necessary capital projects were being delayed because the vision for the industry could not be agreed upon. What had happened, I wondered, to the principles and central purpose of nationalization – the creation of a strategically-important business, operated for the public interest and creating harmony in the workforce?

Industrial relations were seen as a top-down process, rather than – as they should be – bottom up. Work hard at getting things right between management and workers at the places of production, and harmony will flow upwards. The role of the centre is to create a climate in which good industrial relations practices can flourish in the operating unit – not to try and dictate what those practices should be. Having learnt nothing, it seemed to me, from the failures of previous nationalizations, British Steel went down the time-dishonoured route of top-down initiatives. Strong national trade-union leaders met with the central personnel team, including the Chairman and other board members. Negotiations were conducted almost exclusively at this level. National agreements were entered into with enthusiasm, but they had little relevance to the individual steel works.

I am sure that Sir Robert Scholey, the current Chairman of British Steel who has made such a conspicuous success of the human relations and profitability of the business in the 1980s, would judge that one of the milestones in his recovery programme was when he put wage and productivity bargaining back to plant level. This is where it should have been, and this should have been part of the vision of the new British Steel. Regrettably it wasn't. Perhaps in the industrial and political climate of the day it wasn't possible – but I doubt whether it was even recognized at the time as being something important to strive for.

Much time and effort was spent on board structures – experiments were tried with worker-directors. They failed because it was almost impossible to define their role, particularly as it was clear that they represented no one. They were not elected by their fellow workers – nor even appointed by their trade unions.

So British Steel developed, as had many of the earlier nationalized industries, into a prime example of conflict between management and labour. There was little evidence of management and workers trying in harmony to create an enterprise to serve the nation. Nationalization had merely taken the ownership and ultimate control away from private investors, and had passed it on to the politicians. Government ministers are so ephemeral that as ever the role of ownership came to rest in the unwilling hands of the Civil Servants.

The division I joined was Transport & Shipping, and it was headed by an enthusiastic, driving and enjoyable man called Bill Menzies-Wilson. He encouraged enterprise, was participative up to a point, had a touch of the autocrat when needed, but, above all, he wanted to get improvements through action. He was another man who was better respected by those who worked for him than those above, whose political manoeuvrings he found hard to live with. He left BSC shortly after I did to tackle the problems of the redirection of the Ocean Shipping Group, which he did with no little success. We have remained friends ever since, and today he is on the board of NFC as an independent director. 'Independent' aptly describes the stance he has always taken. The tasks that faced the Transport & Shipping Group which I headed were challenging and important.

We calculated that BSC spent something in excess of £200m a year just moving around raw materials and finished products. In fact, there was no shortage of savings to be made. At the simplest level, we found by comparing the road haulage rate schedules of the various works that for essentially the same job, one works could be paying fifty per cent higher charges than another. As a result of the simple act of publishing a league table, it was surprising how quickly the worst performers started to move up the batting order.

When I arrived, there were no fewer than six schemes being canvassed for building deep-water ports for the importation of iron ore. Everyone knew that the deep-water port was a sprat to catch a mackerel. The cost of assembling raw materials for the blast furnace was a significant part of the total cost of making iron. Every works pitching to have its iron and steel-making facilities upgraded knew it would steal a march if it had a local deep-water port at which to berth the super ore carriers. We painstakingly evaluated every scheme, built computer models to analyse the data and simulate the operations, and concluded that the UK needs for raw material imports could be handled from two deep-water ports. The political in-fighting against this recommendation was a new experience in my business life. In the end I am afraid politics not economics won, and it was finally decided to build four – two more than were actually needed, even to this day.

Similar battles were being fought on other aspects of transport and shipping. Some we won: for example, a standardized mineral-carrying rail wagon was agreed on. Some we half won; the operation of the shipping fleet was rationalized. Others we lost – we failed to develop a sensible policy for controlling the export of steel and directing it through specialist ports. But it was a busy time and as a central department we were at least able to draw up a cost-benefit analysis of our work and to demonstrate that we had certainly saved BSC large sums of money. The work was rewarding and we were an enthusiastic team, but there was little emotional satisfaction from observing how minimally the newly-formed BSC was fulfilling its wider responsibility either in its attitude towards its workforce, or in the strategic context of the interests of the nation. It seemed to have learnt nothing from the past failures of other nationalized industries, and it was hard to distinguish any sense of social purpose in the decisions which were being taken. I felt I now wanted to move on and to see if some of the lessons I had learnt along the way could be applied to a business where I was actually accountable for its total success.

Up until now I had been playing supporting roles to others who were taking the real decisions. I was therefore delighted when I was asked by NFC to join them as boss of the largest subsidiary, BRS. It was a nationalized business. Could I make some of my ill-formed theories work in a state-owned environment? The challenge was irresistible.

I received a telephone call from Len Payne who was the boss

of BRS. He was a small, stocky, energetic man with a reputation for ruthless action. He had been tackling the inertia of the largest company in NFC for the last five years. During that time he had sorted out, mainly through redundancies and closures, most of the loss-making depots in the BRS network. He was an accountant and he saw the need to cut the cost base of the business. He did this to great effect. To reduce manning he needed the support of the trade union officers and also the key shop stewards in the depots. He spent much time with them, meeting in pubs and hotels, seeking to persuade, cajole or bully them into giving up restrictive practices. A number of the union officials and shop stewards had his private phone number in the office, which meant they could always contact him direct.

I had met Len on a number of occasions when I was head of transport for British Steel. I was one of his major customers. He invited me to give a lecture to his senior management conference. I felt like Daniel in the lions' den as I addressed them. Remember, I was the man who simply by publishing the different road haulage rates had been able to achieve remarkable reductions in the cost of BSC's road transport bill. BRS were the leading lights in setting the rate tariffs in most of the local areas where steel was produced. On one occasion I went with him to south Wales, where BRS were the major steel carrier and I was less than happy with the transport service his local depot was giving to us. Before my eyes Len filleted the district manager. When he had left, it fell to me, the customer, to pour three large whiskies down the manager's throat to revive him!

There are many stories which illustrate Len Payne's plain speaking and ability to deliver a clear-cut message. At one management conference he sat everyone at the dinner in order of profit return on investment, the manager with the highest return being next to him – the one with the lowest return barely finding a place in the room. He then asked everyone to shake hands with his neighbour, adding that it might be the last chance to get to know him since if profits did not improve at least half of them would not be there next year. It was a direct, hard message that he had to get over – and necessary in a business in which a great deal of lethargy and inertia had developed under state ownership since the 1950s.

I was surprised, therefore, to receive his call. He wanted someone to take over BRS from him as he had been promoted to the NFC headquarters to be Development Director with the particular responsibility of internationalizing the business. After a number of interviews I was offered the job by Sir Daniel Pettit, the Chairman of NFC, who had been brought up in Unilever and who had helped me as a trainee when he was the Chairman of SPD, Unilever's distribution company.

On 2 January 1972 I arrived at the headquarters of BRS. It was located on the sixth and seventh floors of an ugly modern office block in north London. The reception area and the offices were drab with the fading elegance and inspirational design of an Inland Revenue office! Indeed, on the floor below there was an Inland Revenue office!

In the early weeks I had moments of panic. This was my first real command. I was responsible for a business with over nine thousand vehicles which employed over eleven thousand people spread throughout the UK. Would the theories that I had assembled about how to manage a business work in reality? It was also disconcerting to find that the BRS management seemed to take for granted that I knew the answers to their business problems that had been with them for many years. After all, why else had I been appointed? It seemed inadequate to respond to their questions of 'What do you propose to do?' with a question of 'What would you do?' In fact, the solution to most problems can usually be found somewhere in the business; my role was to provide the environment in which the answer is encouraged to emerge.

I decided (and this is not bad advice for all MDs appointed to any business from outside) to spend four to six months trying to evaluate the strengths and weaknesses of BRS. I set forth to visit and listen. In those months I managed to cover all but four of the 120 depots, I had face-to-face interviews with all the senior management. I had forum meetings frequently over dinner with all the branch managers. I spoke with hundreds of drivers, fitters and clerks. During this time I disturbed nothing, allowing the business to run on its existing management systems and methods. Of course, I was itching to get involved and to bring my own theories into practice, but I decided that I had to be as sure as possible that any policies I would promulgate, and any new reorganization I would propose, was relevant, would last and was within the capacity of the people in the business to implement. As I wandered around, Jack Mather who was the Deputy Managing Director (and who subsequently played a vital part in the regeneration of not just BRS but the whole of NFC) used to refer to the process as 'Cobbett's rural rides'.

I knew it was important to assess the people I needed to lead the business for the future. For example, I spent a week with one district manager who was unable to find his way to his own depots – as we lost our way to yet another of his locations, he muttered, 'It's funny, that motorway was not there last time I came!' Another of our managers, Ron Irons, who subsequently became the boss of the whole of BRS, was on the point of leaving to join a private waste disposal business. He had become disillusioned with the centralized management process. After two days – including a hilarious night in a local pub I knew well in Dorset – we mutually concluded we could work together. He tore up his letter of appointment for the new job.

At the end of that six months I drew up the balance sheet of strengths and weaknesses. The strengths were:

a management and workforce which was sound, reliable and thirsty for success

a national network of depots

a wide customer base but one which tended to use us as a last resort; they knew BRS had the resources to handle peak surges of demand which their own fleets or the smaller hauliers could not handle

a good operating, administration and personnel management system

they had started to realize the importance of marketing, but it was in the embryo stage

The weaknesses outnumbered the strengths, but all were clear and all were soluble through time – but it would be a long haul.

There was no sign of strategic or corporate planning – there was no clear-cut vision for the business.

45

BRS was very centralized. All decisions were taken at headquarters in Whetstone. If there was a problem a senior manager from HQ would come and sort it out.

The board and management spent most of its time and efforts in trying to improve the general haulage service. It represented 75 per cent of the turnover and it made no money – and probably never would because the small haulier with negligible overheads and higher personal productivity could always do the basic job of moving full loads better and cheaper than we could.

Its best chance of success was with contract hire, where BRS provided a customer with a vehicle or fleet of vehicles with or without drivers for the customer to use as he decided. The contract was usually for five years and the profit was more or less guaranteed. However, this was receiving only a small part of management's attention. Indeed, when I arrived the company was being split into two, with 75 per cent of management effort being directed totally to general haulage and 25 per cent going into a separate contract business.

Entrepreneurial flair was lacking. The majority of projects were rejected because they were not professionally presented, rather than because of their lack of intrinsic business merit. Consequently, there had been almost no major investment or development in the business other than vehicle replacement for many years. The department in headquarters responsible for evaluating development projects was affectionately known as the 'project prevention' department.

The solutions that emerged were, in fact, simple and obvious, and I am pleased to say that most of the systems and methods installed in 1972 still exist today.

First and foremost we had to reduce the influence of the centre on operational and personnel matters. To do this we created seven regional companies. Their job was to face the customers, sell the services to them, and to ensure that their employees were well motivated and that their operations were efficient. Each company employed a little over a thousand people. They were about the right size for one man – the new company MD – to get his arms around. He could know all his people and all his major customers. There was nothing scientific or magical in the number of regions we created – it just happened that we had seven managers who I thought had the necessary flair and skill to lead the new companies. Or, perhaps I should say six. The seventh was Ron Fortune, and I remember saying to him on his appointment, 'I don't think you are good enough, but I am not sure you are not.' Hardly the best way of presenting someone with a major responsibility, but I hoped it would make him determined to show me that I was wrong to doubt his ability.

He took over North Eastern BRS and it was losing money. He soon put a stop to that nonsense and today he runs a successful, growing and forward-looking business. He proved to have great determination and stamina – the qualities that are the most difficult to spot!

The role of headquarters had to be reduced, but given more focus. I was inclined to close the second floor and curtail the staff to within a single storey. I remember Robert Townsend in *Up the Organization* putting forward the idea that the size of any HQ will depend on the number of chairs that are available. My aim was therefore to halve the number of seats – and this we just about managed to do. Whilst dropping its operational role, I wanted headquarters to become the powerhouse for product and service development, and for formulating the vision of the future. It would also agree targets with the companies, allocate capital, and monitor performance.

To ensure that headquarters took into account the views of the new companies, a group policy committee was set up on which sat the MDs of the new companies and the headquarters specialists.

In order to help me with the long-term direction of the business I poached (for the first and only time in my career) a manager from another company. Clive Beattie had worked with me in British Steel and was responsible for the Transport and Shipping development. He was an unusual man. Trained in operational research, he had written a book on managing research which was published before he was thirty. When we first met, we had a row about British Steel's approach to iron ore importation. We have rowed frequently ever since. But he has an off-beat mind, capable of original thought, and an off-beat lifestyle to go with it. I knew I wanted him to help me put vision and flair into a conventional business. So I poached him – a practice I don't really approve of, but needs must if the devil drives. The initial reactions of the middle-aged conventional managers of BRS to this long-haired, guitar-playing planner were less than enthusiastic, but they soon came to respect his skills.

Another major cultural change I brought about was to make it perfectly clear that however much they enjoyed 'playing trucks' – which is how I described General Haulage – I was not going to join them. I was only interested in services and products that had a chance of making money. So whereas board meetings and management conferences had in the past been dominated by never-ending discussions about trunk services and sheets and ropes (who stole whose sheets and who failed to replace whose ropes), we would henceforth talk only about the products of the future – contract hire, warehousing, distribution and truck rental. You may think this foolhardy when 75 per cent of the turnover was represented by General Haulage, but I somehow had to move it away from centre stage so that we could concentrate upon our real product strengths.

The final culture change was to throw away the rule book. There was an elaborate system of central instructions which told everyone exactly what to do in any situation. I told the new company management that they were now accountable, and it was their business to do what seemed sensible. I wanted to liberate initiative and action. We did not burn the management manuals, but we did get rid of them. If you want someone to be accountable, you have to minimize the restrictions put upon him – otherwise he has a great armoury of excuses as to why he could not achieve.

For example, a road haulier's tool of trade is the truck. Trucks had in the past been bought centrally because an extra 2½ per cent discount could then be obtained. To a greater or lesser degree the wishes of the operator on truck selection were listened to in the centre. I decided to do away with this system. In future the individual companies would decide what trucks they should buy and get on with buying them. We may have lost a 2½ per cent discount, but it eliminated the excuse put forward for not making budget that the trucks which the company owned were not selected by operational management. If you believe in accountability, you must remove as many restrictions to performance as possible.

Meanwhile I had my private telephone number in the office changed. It was no part of our decentralized management style for shop stewards to have direct access to me.

The first major test of the new devolved system appeared within three months. Yet another Transport Act had come into force which required all drivers of large trucks to be in possession of a heavy goods vehicle licence. In the Birmingham area the local Transport & General Workers' Union leader was a man named Allan Law. He was militant, powerful, with an authority over his men which was akin to a teamster union boss in the USA. He controlled the Birmingham area – nobody operated road transport in that area without having first come to some agreement with him.

He decided that the employers should pay a premium to any driver who held an HGV licence. The employers argued that it was a necessary licence to do the job and hence did not warrant a special payment. Law decided to have the confrontation with the newly-established Midlands BRS company. He called all the drivers out on strike behind the banner of '£3 a week for an HGV'. Historically this issue would have been handled at headquarters; I was determined the issue should be resolved locally, otherwise the whole concept of devolving responsibility for industrial relations to the new companies would fail at the first hurdle.

The strike lasted four weeks. Bets were taken that in the end I would have to settle it by direct negotiation with Allan Law. That I would not do. Finally our drivers, particularly outside Birmingham, recognized that Law's demands were not going to be met and they went back to work. It had cost the new company over £1m in lost profit but it established devolved authority as a reality.

During the dispute I was constantly getting calls from our competitors saying how important it was that we should not concede. If we did, it would mean that the whole haulage industry would also have to pay for the HGV licence. We had to try and find alternative ways of moving our customers' goods and we sought the help of our competitors. When the strike finished not a single competitor handed back our business. So much for honour amongst competitors!

One of the most important developments over my four years with BRS was the introduction of the annual planning programme. I wanted to ensure that time was spent not only in looking back at results but also forward at tasks that needed to be accomplished. The annual cycle went like this: in spring each company carried out its review of strategy. This was a mind-expanding process involving few figures (we tried to keep the accountants at bay during these sessions as figures tend to constrain rather than expand horizons). The review ensured that we focused on the future. In summer we drew up the three-year plan, which was a much more disciplined approach, and, within the constraints of cash and management ability, we sought to plot in some detail the path down which we needed to go towards the distant horizon. It was a top-down, bottom-up exercise. We in the centre told the companies what we could afford and what we thought they were capable of achieving. They told us what they needed and what they thought they could do. Reconciliation of the two sides was what produced a credible plan.

In autumn the first year of the plan was re-examined in great depth and became the budget for the following year. Eventually the achievement of budget became the only touchstone of success. In the early years we tended to concentrate not so much on what had been promised in the budget but how much better we were doing than the previous year.

The ability to assess what a business is capable of achieving in the future is probably the most difficult management skill to acquire – it took five or six years before we felt we were sufficiently sophisticated to use forecasting as the real test of attainment.

Looking back, I have to admit we did not make much progress in the motivation of the drivers, fitters and clerks. It was difficult enough to get the management up to scratch. Devolving authority not only to the new companies but beyond that into the individual depots meant having to change managers from being operators of resources to being businessmen. This entailed a programme of almost individual coaching. David White, MD of Eastern BRS, volunteered his company to act as the guinea pig. He is one of the most effective managers I have ever known. Though White by name, he is black and white by nature. He believes that in order to manage successfully, you must be able to give clear-cut objectives to those you manage. Most issues are simple and should not be made complex. In many ways he is right; but his style tended to clash with my view that it is not necessary to spray the solutions on the wall. If you present a sensible person with the facts, he will generally reach the right conclusions without having to be given precise instructions. Nonetheless, David White's style produced results and people enjoyed working for him because they knew exactly what they had to achieve.

David White took over from me at BRS, and eventually became Deputy Chairman of NFC. He was a great supporter of the employee buy-out some five years later. He was famous for management instructions like, 'Don't argue, sunshine, just have half of your business in contract hire in two years' time.'

He and his team, with an outside consultant called Jim Easton, set about trying to convert mature, dour, dyed-in-the-wool depot managers into businessmen with a modicum of local entrepreneurial flair. The alternative was to get rid of them all and start again with new managers. We preferred to try to re-train and re-focus. There were successes and failures, but it did enable us to realize what changes we needed to make in skills and attitudes if we were to be successful in pushing authority downwards.

One notable triumph was an old stager called Arthur Hopwood who managed our depot at Knottingley. As part of the training everyone had to develop a long-term plan for his own depot. I visited him about five years later and he proudly showed me the plan he had drawn up to change his depot from being 80 per cent dependent upon General Haulage to having a balanced mix of contract hire, truck rental, warehousing, engineering, with General Haulage down to only 30 per cent of the revenue. 'There you are, governor,' he said. 'I have done it and I can retire a happy man.' He was a fine example of what can be achieved by a mature manager if you can only lift his eyes out of the mud of day-to-day problems and let him focus on a more distant vision.

But managing in a nationalized industry was more difficult

than it need be. The media did not help – it was almost as if they wanted the businesses which we owned in common to fail. God knows, it was difficult enough getting private industry to use our services because there was no one who believed that a nationalized business could be customer orientated. Those customers that we had we needed to cherish.

Like many private-sector companies, we arranged a special social event once a year to which we invited our major customers and their wives. One year we planned a dinner and dance at Belvoir Castle – one of the English stately homes in Rutland. The *Daily Express* got hold of the story – it would not have been a story at all had we been a private company. Here was a state-owned business wasting the nation's money, they said. The headlines burst forth: 'Junketing in the Castle'! Of course, the trade unions felt that they should also join in the general condemnation of management 'wasting' money on entertaining customers. So they threatened to picket the event. It was difficult to decide whether or not we should cancel the whole affair and bow down under the weight of unfair criticism. 'Do what's right and shame the devil' – so we carried on and had a great evening well enjoyed by the customers. But it was an early example to me of what is sauce for the private enterprise goose but not necessarily for the nationalized gander.

We always had the problem of knowing how to reward success. The pay scales of management were depressed by government controls. How to keep our top management team motivated while palpably underpaying them was to become an increasing problem. I decided that the route forward should try to create an atmosphere of fun and friendship among senior management. It was also particularly important to include wives in whatever we were doing socially. We badly needed them on our side, because to underpay and expect long working hours from their husbands was only to encourage spouse antagonism towards the company. So we involved them in our customer entertainment. We organized a ladies' committee, which my wife chaired, to plan the major customer event each year.

If we had a good year, the only way we could reward was to arrange for a conference in pleasant surroundings where, although we did some business, in the main it was a social event with us all enjoying a relaxing weekend together. Some years later, after BRS had had a really excellent year, David White rewarded the board and their wives by taking them for a long weekend to the Canaries. A Conservative MP heard of this and made a major issue of it in the House of Commons. This unfair publicity made us reluctant in the future to give motivational rewards, which are normal incentives in the private sector.

Slowly the BRS super tanker began to turn. It was not an overnight success story, but year after year the quality of the business improved. The profits grew and new services and initiatives started to flow. Truck Rental was introduced and we became market leaders within two or three years; BRS Rescue – an emergency recovery service for heavy trucks – was launched, warehousing was built; Distribution services were sold; Contract Hire grew as each and every depot was required to offer it, and General Haulage declined. Instead of being a whore standing on the street corner waiting for customers to use our services as and when *they* wanted, we slowly changed the relationship to that of a mistress which meant longer-term commitment. Ultimately the relationship with the customers became a marriage involving mutual dependence as a result of the product thrust of BRS into Contract Hire and Distribution.

Above all the four years I had with BRS were fun. The top group developed a great bond and we enjoyed each other's company. A surprising number of us were golfers, or perhaps more accurately played golf. In 1973 a weekend of golf was suggested. The prime mover who organized that first golfing weekend was the waspish Harry Cliff, a Yorkshireman who ran the car transporting operation. He was a good operator with not much time for committees, strategy or business analysis. He had the ability of bringing us all down to earth. On one occasion we had spent much time debating a marketing problem: 'If only the customer was more receptive' . . . 'if only the manufacturers would deliver the trucks on time . . .'

'If only, if only . . .' Harry exploded, 'if only my aunt had balls she would have been my uncle!'

The golf weekend was held at Aberdovey in north Wales where there was a first-class course and where Eric Shortland, the MD of Mortons BRS, who had a little more of the world's wealth than the rest of us, owned a weekend cottage. It was designed to sleep five comfortably. Regularly twice a year twelve of us somehow managed to cram ourselves in. The atmosphere of good living, friendship and laughter that Eric created is something that all of us valued. There was little business talk, in fact it was positively discouraged, but there was much golf, eating and drinking. Brian Hayward, a giant of a man who was in charge of one of the BRS companies, cooked the main meal, while others acted as vintner, sauce maker, social secretary, sergeant-at-arms. We had all the offices covered. My role was to cook the breakfast and to lead the singing. This was the kind of environment in which, a number of years later, the first thoughts of an employee buy-out of NFC from the government were formulated.

Many people think that, as boss, you should not make friends with, or have social contact with, your business colleagues as it may colour your judgement or undermine your leadership. In theory this may be true; in practice I found it wasn't. I cannot remember a single occasion when anyone in the golfing society tried to take advantage of our friendship, nor was I prevented from having to take action against two or three of the group who did not achieve their business objectives. What I do know is that the friendships helped to keep a talented team together when we were short of other means of motivating them.

The BRS management were an earthy, happy lot. The first management conference I attended as their boss was in Harrogate. I decided to go to bed early as I wasn't yet sufficiently sure of my relationship with them all to participate fully in the late night revelry. I had a bar in my room and I had just dropped off to sleep when the door burst open and a figure marched in, grabbed the bottle of whisky and made off into the night. I never did find out who it was. Perhaps someone will send me a replacement bottle with a written confession!

At the same conference two of the managers who we were encouraging to become entrepreneurs went out to the local night club and persuaded two of the strippers to come back and do a late-night show. The finance director was put in charge of collecting the money to pay the girls. He knew what the girls were to be paid, he knew how many spectators would be attending. He fixed the entrance fee and yet he still managed to make a loss. It was not an encouraging start to the campaign to make each manager a profitable businessman!

I have found throughout my business life that humour is a great lubricant. It helps smooth the way for less popular policies, and it calms anger. A sense of humour is one of the ingredients that I look for in any good leader, and NFC is blessed that most of its managers possess it in full measure.

In the meantime our parent company, the National Freight Corporation, was having a rough time. A number of things had gone wrong, all at the same time. 'When sorrows come, they come not single spies but in battalions.' The major setbacks were in the two Parcels businesses and the European ventures. Their losses absorbed the profits that BRS and Pickfords were making and pushed NFC into operating losses of over £16m in 1975, with losses, after extraordinary items and interest, of £31m in 1975. Interest was a large burden because nationalized industries were financed totally by debt with fixed interest payments to be made each year. There was no 'equity' capital. I remember Dan Pettit likened the system to medieval usury – if a nationalized business lost money it had to borrow to pay the losses and so next year its interest burden was that much higher. Each year the mountain to climb to reach bottom-line profitability became steeper. Eventually, of course, the debt had to be written off. There was no such thing as shareholder funds taking the strain in the bad years.

However, some of the problems were self-inflicted. It was clear that at some stage the two major parcels businesses, National Carriers and BRS Parcels, had to be merged and remotivated. You may well remember the horses and carts doing local deliveries with the driver's dog on the back protecting the load – that was the forefather of NCL. And some may remember that BRS Parcels was the company that transported their school trunks at the beginning and end of terms.

The problem was that two powerful unions – the NUR who organized NCL and TGWU who organized BRS Parcels – opposed the merger. In the early years of the NFC, BRS Parcels were the major profit earner – but this was in the days before competition from the newly emerging private sector of road haulage following the liberalization of entry brought about by the 1968 Transport Act. Competition initially took the form of price-cutting coupled with superior services being offered. BRS Parcels' profitability quickly disappeared. NCL had never been profitable, in fact it lost £25m on a £25m turnover in 1969. I think this might earn it a place in the *Guinness Book of Records*. The improvements achieved in the early days of NFC were not maintained when the recession of 1974/75 hit the economy. A number of attempts were made to merge the two companies. Faced with union opposition each time, NFC backed away. Consequently losses mounted.

Observing this in the comfort of knowing that the problem was not my direct responsibility, I concluded that you must never start on a course of action unless you are prepared to see it through to the end, regardless of the cost. To back away leads to management demotivation. The only reason why management should ever have to back away is because they have failed to analyse thoroughly the problem in advance. Frequently, the reaction of the major players affected is not anticipated. If management is seeking change, they must do a great deal of homework to avoid the risk of their plans being thwarted. The greater the business problem, the more homework is required to be done.

The other problem was Europe. Sir Dan Pettit's vision was of NFC being as large and important in Europe as it was in the UK within five years. He was faced with the concept of a single European market and he recognized that a distribution business which could offer to a manufacturing company a solution to the problems of serving their customers throughout the Common Market would have a clear-cut marketing edge. The vision was right; but as with all visions it is the timing and execution of the strategy that is critical. Aiming for rapid growth, a top-heavy European group was formed. The idea was to establish distribution depots on green field sites, in selected areas which would act as 'explosion' points from which goods from the UK would be delivered into Europe.

This was the slow route and, driven by the need for more rapid expansion, acquisitions were sought. The acquisition strategy was to buy cheaply companies that were not performing well, and, by the use of British management (which itself was not performing too well in the UK), turn the companies round. So a large, unprofitable freight forwarder was bought in Germany, two bulk tanker companies and a refrigerated transport business in France. A minority stake was also bought in a car transporting business in France. It was a formula for disaster.

The operations started from green field sites made losses in the early years, and it was inevitable that they would. The acquired companies, in particular the two tanker companies, were affected by the downturn in the economy brought about by the oil crisis. British management was not strong enough to cope with the turnaround required in a hostile market place. As the losses grew, so the Conservatives in opposition seized on the political ammunition that the mounting losses presented. What was a state-owned company doing using tax payers' money to buy European companies? asked Norman Fowler, the Shadow Transport Secretary. It was a question which the Labour government found hard to answer in the face of such poor performances.

They looked for a political solution – at least one that would enable Bill Rodgers, the Minister for Transport, to stand before parliament with a fig leaf to cover an otherwise bare body. The solution to the £31m losses announced early in 1976 was management changes at the top. The proposal was to bring more executives on to the main board and to separate the roles of chairman and chief executive. In keeping with many of the boards of the nationalized industries at the time, NFC had a mainly non-executive board, with the principal executives attending from time to time to report on their stewardship.

The natural choice for Chief Executive would have been my predecessor at BRS, Len Payne. However, as a result of frustration on the one hand at the lack of tough central management in NFC, and an offer he could hardly refuse on the other, he left to become the logistics director for Sainsbury's. Sainsbury's gain was NFC's loss as he proved to be an outstanding Distribution Director. The food retail industry paid him the compliment of copying the composite distribution depot concept which he first invented and which put Sainsbury's ahead of the field.

The choice therefore fell on me. I was initially designated Vice

Chairman Operations. I was to look after the present while another executive looked after the future – a management precept which cannot make sense. When a chief executive is driving the current operations forward, he must do so with an eye to the vision of the future which he at least shares, and to which he has contributed.

But there was so much to do to stop the bleeding that there was no time for management theory. I was invited to join the board and requested to take a small salary cut. In future my salary would be determined by the government salary review board and not by NFC. The government believed that salaries paid to executives in the nationalized industries should be comparable to, and preferably below, the earnings of the civil servants to whom they effectively reported. The idea that what an individual earns is determined by the market for his skills had not yet entered the official credo. So I took a cut of salary in exchange for a better pension – not the best way of motivating a 47-year-old with three children. Nevertheless, I still wanted to show that a nationalized industry could work. BRS was beginning to be respected by its private sector competitors, so I thought it might work for the whole of NFC.

Almost the first meeting I attended when I took up my new responsibilities was in the office of Sir Idwal Pugh, the Permanent Secretary at the Ministry of Transport and as such the senior civil servant. He was also the accounting officer. This was a role that I had not encountered before but it is an important one. In each ministry the accounting officer, responsible to his minister, to the government and ultimately to parliament, has to ensure that the revenues his ministry spends are properly and wisely dispersed, and for purposes which parliament has agreed. As taxpayers we should be thankful that this role does exist. I would feel a little more comforted if, like the chairman of a public company, the accounting officer could be sacked when the control is less professional than it should be.

My Chairman, the Financial Director and I were dragooned before the Accounting Officer. We were told in sombre official terms that our access to the National Loan Fund had been cut off. Our credit lines had been withdrawn. The brokers were in. If it were possible for a nationalized industry to go into receivership, we had reached that stage. In future, any cash we needed to spend had to be approved by the ministry. Such was the faith that they had in our management that the government, as is the normal response when things go wrong, appointed consultants to crawl all over the business. The remit was to come up with a credible plan for stopping the losses and getting the business on to a sound footing. Not bad for my first day in a new job!

I took the view that with losses in so many parts of the business, I needed all the help I could get. So after a short period of feeling resentful that I had had consultants imposed upon me, I decided that I would make as much use of them as possible. Teams of them were despatched into all the major subsidiaries and they came back with many ideas on how the different parts of the business could be strategically refocused to make them viable.

Three major issues had to be faced. Firstly, the European companies. They had to be disposed of. The opportunity cost in terms of scarce management resource was too great to try to salvage them. Better to concentrate our management skills in getting the home base viable. Secondly, we had to face up to massive redundancies in National Carriers – it was necessary to prune the business right back to get at the inner core which might eventually make money. Thirdly, virtually the whole of the top management team at NFC headquarters needed changing, and some of the managing directors of the subsidiaries too.

After my first month at NFC, the first period's figures were put on my desk on a Friday evening. One subsidiary had lost £1m in the period. I phoned the MD. He said he had not seen the figures and therefore could not immediately comment. I replied that if he knew his business, he wouldn't have to wait for the figures.

You surely must *know* you are making losses of this kind from the antennae that you have. It was this kind of management attitude which was alien to anything I had experienced in BRS that made me realize the top management had to be changed. We did not do it all in a month, but within two years there was no one left at the top of NFC's operational management who had been there when the major losses were incurred. The principle of accountability had to be instilled. I am not proud of this period of crisis management. I am not a hirer and firer. All my instincts are to try to change and retrain. But when the ship is on fire, you haven't the time for participative and caring management. The important thing is to get the old crew that caused the fire off the ship, and get on board a new crew that have the skills to put it out.

I regret having to ask anyone to leave the business. But senior level management failure may mean redundancies among junior staff who were not involved in the decisions which caused the problems. If a man is to be paid well, given status and authority, he must also be prepared to be held accountable. If a senior manager has failed, he must leave his management position. But how he is treated then as an individual is all-important. You can tell as much about a business from the way it treats its failures as you can about a nation from the way it treats its misfits.

For many reasons the next three years were depressing. The only way forward into profit was to take the accountants' route. We had somehow to pull down the cost line of the business. Our major costs were labour. Like many bankers, government was prepared to finance redundancy; but they were less interested in providing capital for new ventures. Who can blame them when their one act of entrepreneurial faith of providing cash for NFC to conquer Europe had gone so badly awry? So we pruned relentlessly. Costs did come down as depots were closed and the number employed was reduced by thousands.

At the same time we sought to find new services which were more sophisticated and had added value. Some were successful, like Fashionflow which was developed to meet the special needs of Marks & Spencer. Some were failures, like Bookflow with which we sought to provide a specialist service for the book trade. This failed, in fact, because of labour problems. The drivers claimed SOGAT membership so that when called by their chapel they could work in Fleet Street. They were able to earn more money in Fleet Street for four hours' work on a Saturday night handling newspapers than working a full week for us delivering books.

Another cause of failure was that the management approach to logistics in the publishing industry was ossified. They resisted our attempts to modernize the distribution of books. It was regarded as an acceptable level of service for an order for an out-of-stock book from a reader to take as long as three weeks to be met. We suggested a system akin to that used by the vehicle repairers when a vehicle is off the road waiting for a spare part to complete its repair. At a special delivery price the spare part can be ordered by computer terminal on the central stock and be delivered within twenty-four hours. The publishers took the view that it would not enhance sales, book customers were quite happy with the 21-day service they were getting. I am sure that there is seldom an industrial relations problem without some fault in the management being present too.

We recognized the need to develop new products. Truck Rentals was launched by BRS. Within Pickfords Removals there lurked an underdeveloped travel retail business which was being run as a part-time activity by Household Removals managers. We decided to give it air by separating it from its parent. We put in a management that would give it the full-time attention and expertise it needed. Today it is the second largest retail travel business in the UK. We launched a national commercial vehicle breakdown service to provide for the truck owner the same service that the AA and RAC give to car owners.

We had fun but no profit from starting a branded plumbing service. The best that could be said for it was that it had an eye-catching name – 'Summers the Plumbers'. It failed because we did not understand the plumbing business, and it taught us a lesson about sticking to our knitting! In future we should only develop services in the areas where we had the skills and knowledge. Although, even to this day, we do from time to time indulge in a little new venturing without risking too much. Despite what the textbooks say, without some attempt to break new ground a business can become pretty dull.

Slowly the losses were staunched and with the aid of interest-free capital grants for National Carriers we began to improve the operating profit. Over £100m of debt was written off which allowed our interest payments to be reduced. Consequently, bottom-line profitability came into sight. It was also a period when the economy was expanding, and inflation was running wild, and it is always easier to make profits in this environment.

61

In the meantime, Sir Daniel Pettit had retired as Chairman, and I had hopes of being his successor after all the effective work that the new team had put in. But the choice fell on Bobbie Lawrence who was the Deputy Chairman of British Rail and a non-executive director of NFC. It was a pretty insensitive appointment – since nationalization British Rail had always lost money. National Carriers (which had come to us from British Rail), through its persistent losses, had been in part responsible for our bankruptcy. We had spent much time and effort refocusing the ex-BR employees in NFC towards commercial and financial objectives. British Rail still had a subsidy mentality. This kind of attitude was what NFC was seeking to put behind it. Yet the government appointed a railwayman to preside over us. I had a heated meeting with the Secretary of State, Bill Rodgers, when he told me of his choice.

In the event Bobbie Lawrence's appointment was an excellent one. He was a very unusual railwayman. He was pragmatic, entrepreneurial, a horse dealer and a trader. He understood government and knew when to leave well alone and when to interfere. We were both strong-willed individuals and it was widely assumed that we would be unable to work together. However, we formed a fine partnership built upon mutual respect. We became great friends, which stood us in great stead through the later buy-out years when Bobbie Lawrence had to represent the interests of the existing owners – the government – whereas I was seeking the best deal for the new owners – the workforce.

But on reflection it was hardly surprising that I was not chosen to be Chairman. Some eighteen months earlier, when inflation was accelerating fast, for the third year in succession government decided that it had to hold down the salaries of all senior political appointees, and this included the board members of the nationalized industries. Having accepted a salary cut to join the board, my purchasing power had subsequently been eroded annually. Things were getting desperate at home. The children were all of school age and were being educated in private schools, but I had to take the girls out of the private system as I just could not afford the school fees. So, while my responsibilities were expanding at work, the standard of living at home was declining. This was another example of how government fails to realize the importance of motivating the senior executives in the industries they control. I decided to leave NFC. I resigned, reluctantly, and was surprised at the reaction of the board who in the main were non-executives and from private industry. They sympathized with the stance I was taking, and suggested that all I needed to do was resign from the board but remain as an executive. They still wanted me to be Chief Executive. Once I was no longer a board member, the government's control over my salary and employment package evaporated. They would pay me a fair rate for the job. They would invite me to attend all board meetings and would still regard me as an equal when key decisions had to be taken.

This was the outcome, but it did not endear me to the Labour politicians – so perhaps this had something to do with my not getting the promotion that I felt my commercial performance had justified. In the end it turned out well. Bobbie Lawrence dealt with the politicians and I was left free to deal with the business.

Good performance against the strategic plan pushed NFC closer and closer to overall profitability. The plan was fairly simple stuff. We had to get out of Europe for which the government was prepared to pick up that bill; severely prune the big loss-maker National Carriers; and reduce our dependence on low-margin parcel activities which were full of restrictive practices. At the same time we needed to enlarge the parts of the business where we had some competitive advantage – household removals, contract hire, travel and dedicated distribution for major clients – and to innovate and attack new markets, such as waste management, truck rental, and national breakdown services. But, although we now had good product strategy, I was conscious that we were not really doing much to remotivate the management and staff.

At about the time that I was nursing my disappointment at not being appointed Chairman, Arthur Smith, the Managing Director of Roadline – one of the parcels operations – had been selected to go on a management course run by the American Management Association. It was a general mid-career course which was attended by all our potential board members. Some went to Stanford, others IMEDE. Arthur Smith had decided to go on the AMA course. They always held these courses for chief executives at top-class locations. It was mainly Americans who attended, and the costs were tax deductible. So they were held in places like Gleneagles Hotel in Scotland; Villa d'Este Hotel on Lake Como, Italy, and Hilton Head Island in the US. This particular course was held at the Penina, a fine golf hotel in the Algarve. The course had been designed by Henry Cotton who lived there himself. At the last minute Arthur Smith had to cry off. The course was paid for – so I decided to go and have a week's golf at the company's expense to see if I could cheer myself up. When I arrived, I felt in all decency that I should attend the opening business session. I was captivated. They expounded a system for managing a business which rationalized all the various unconnected theories and experiences that I had acquired through the years.

It brought together for me vision and purpose; with motivation and remuneration. It preached the participative management style. Like all good things, it was simple. Everyone should have a plan and with it a vision of the future. The chairman's plan might have a ten-year horizon, the loading bank supervisors' only a six-month horizon. The vision should be capable of being encapsulated into a single statement – the mission statement. The best example of a mission statement is the one that President Kennedy gave to the National Aeronautic and Space Administration when he said, 'This nation should commit itself to achieving the goal before the decade is out of landing a man on the moon and returning him safely to earth.' Everyone who worked on the space programme, and the many support programmes, knew exactly what it was that had to be achieved. Somehow NFC have never managed to produce a mission statement with quite that level of flair – but we keep trying.

From this vision/plan a number of tasks emerge that have to be achieved if the mission is to be successful. These tasks become key objectives. They are agreed with your boss. At the same time as the objectives are agreed, a remuneration deal is struck. 'You do this for the company and this is what the company will do for you.' This was an eye-opener for me as the accepted wisdom at the time was firstly, that it was unwise to link the salary review too closely with achievement, and secondly, it was imprudent to commit to a remuneration deal in advance because so many things can go wrong.

The deal that was struck between the employee and the boss in turn leads to appraisal. We had sought to introduce appraisals into NFC in the mid-1970s. Only by appraising an individual can his weaknesses be identified, and a suitable training programme be devised to improve his performance as a manager. Appraisals also give the boss an important opportunity to acknowledge an individual's success, and equally important, give the employee a chance to air his views on the way he is being managed.

We had all attended courses on the art of appraising and they involved role acting. I remember one of the highlights was the performance of Ron Fortune, the Managing Director of North-Eastern BRS. He was being appraised by one of his colleagues at a training session. He walked in and before his appraiser could say anything he said, 'By the way, sir, your usual salmon is in the car boot!'

Much later, when Ron Fortune was carrying out the appraisals himself, Arthur Hopwood was attending his first appraisal. He stumped into the office (he suffered badly from arthritis) and said, 'Now, governor, there are two things I want from this appraisal. The first is a large whisky and the second is a big salary increase as I shall be retiring soon.'

Ron Fortune responded, 'The first is easy,' and poured out a large whisky for both of them, 'but the second is more difficult.' However, after two or three more large whiskies the second objective was also achieved!

At another training session we asked one of our less subtle colleagues to handle with sensitivity the early retirement of one of his managers because of inadequate performance. 'Be subtle, broach the issue delicately,' we counselled.

'Come in Shortland,' he said. 'Sit down. Now we are here to see how we can phase you out!'

But the introduction of appraisal did not prove totally successful. Some managers saw it as 'playing God', and felt it was not up to one human being to tell another his faults. However, our policy of promising a payment deal in advance meant that appraisal was almost inevitable if someone failed to meet the objectives. If you promise someone 10 per cent merit increase for a high performance and you award him only 2½ per cent, you have got an appraisal on your hands whether you like it or not.

Finally, the AMA philosophy taught me that you would only get good people to work well with you if you involve them in key decisions before they are taken. Authoritarian management works and can be perfectly effective if the authoritarian manager is good. But in this day and age, the educated young manager is not going to work indefinitely for an autocrat who is unwilling to consult or explain. Before any manager takes a decision, he must consult with those who will be affected by it. As I've said, if the ship is sinking you cannot be participative. You issue the orders and everyone must comply. But the majority of business is not about 'sinking ships' – it is about searching for competitive advantage and improvement. Participation and involvement is vital if you are to maximize the contribution to excellence of the entire workforce.

So I returned from Penina with my golf clubs all but unused. I had attended every business session and I was now clear how I wanted NFC to be managed and what culture and values the business should have. All the pieces in the jigsaw had slotted into place.

When I arrived back, I summoned my colleagues and revealed all to them. Initially the reaction was predictable: 'How many courses have you been on in your life, Peter?'

'Well, actually, apart from my early training with Unilever this is the first course.' The reply was greeted with a knowing chuckle from the well-experienced course attendees among my colleagues. 'He's been sold a pup on his first visit to the kennels' was their all-too-obvious reaction. I made them an offer. 'Go on this course in the next three or four months and, when you return, we will meet again and see if we have a blueprint for the management style we should adopt in the future.' There was little objection – they all knew the excellent watering holes that

AMA chose for their chief executive courses. Four months later we reassembled and agreed it was the right style and the right way to try to manage the business in the future.

It was not going to be easy. Road haulage seems to breed self-made autocrats and authoritarian managers. Many of our managers saw this to be the style practised by many of the most successful operations in the private sector. But we were determined to change that culture. Many man years were spent putting over the participative style of management. Each manager throughout NFC over the next three or four years was subjected to the same programme of training as the board, and more than £1m was spent trying to get the participative style of management firmly embedded at all levels of NFC. Even today, some ten years later, I would be deceiving myself if I believed that we have banished the authoritarian autocrat from the NFC. We haven't. The problem is that so often he is profitable in the short term. But we are slowly getting there.

At the same time as tackling the culture of NFC, we introduced more results-orientated salaries for the managers. In 1976, when I first became Chief Executive, it was a year of high inflation. The total salary 'award' for the year was about 20 per cent. Everyone was given 17½ per cent to protect their salaries against inflation, and only 2½ per cent was available for merit. So the salary difference between the individual who achieved all his objectives and the guy who achieved nothing, was just 2½ per cent. This was not unusual in the nationalized industries; in general salary policy was about 'fairness'. I suppose it was an infection caught from strong trade unions. They believed in and negotiated for 'the rate for the job' – whoever does a job should get the agreed rate. Never mind that no two individuals will ever do any job equally well. One will always be more effective than the other. Anyone going into industry should recognize that winning the commercial war is all about being more effective than the competitor. So what we must look for and recognize is effectiveness – this involves analysis and appraisal. It involves giving the top brick off the chimney to the achiever. The blue-eyed boy syndrome is how some trade unionists would describe a wage package mainly based on appraisal by the boss. Far better in their view to have everyone paid the same – a 'fairer' method. It may be 'fairer', but it is not the way to ensure competitive success.

We also had to break through the existing salary system which started with the evaluation of the job. Once carried out, the evaluation ensured that the individual was guaranteed increases every year as he passed through the appropriate grade. Most Civil Service jobs are rewarded this way even today. We agreed with evaluation. The pace at which an individual increased his standard of living, however, should not be determined by his ability to stay alive and grow older, but by his achievements against his agreed targets. There should be no automatic progression through a 'grade', and we therefore moved away from this system for senior managers in the mid-1970s.

To the new system we added short-term bonusing. It was obvious that NFC would only survive, and hence have the chance of achieving some of its longer-term visions, if it achieved its short-term cash and profit targets. Cash in a disaster is all important – you can make losses for many years and survive but you only run out of cash once. So cash disciplines became central. We decided that if a managing director of a company and his support team achieved budget, they would have 10 per cent of their salary in bonus – but only if they had first achieved their cash targets. If they over-achieved, they could have up to 30 per cent of salary in bonus. Having been summoned to run the NFC when it had just run out of cash, and having suffered the humiliation of close monitoring by government for over two years so that every significant item of expenditure had to be approved by the Department, I was determined never to allow NFC to get into this situation again. Cash was to be king.

So a more results-orientated salary deal was put in place. The new philosophy was that salaries would permanently increase if quality objectives in a plan or mission were achieved, and a one-year bonus would be awarded on the achievement of short-term profit and cash targets.

You can imagine my surprise when my old colleagues on the board of BRS sent messages that they would not accept the new bonus system. I went to see them. They said that I was insulting them if I thought that by offering them a few extra shekels they would work harder. They were working as hard as they could – I should know that – and I should be ashamed of myself for so undervaluing their commitment. They would prefer – if it was all the same to me – to continue to celebrate any successes that collectively they may have by enjoying a weekend away together with their wives. I tried to persuade them that it wasn't harder work I wanted from them but more effective work. I did my best to persuade – I put on my full array of participative skills – but still this group of guys whom I respected enormously was adamant.

So at the outset of the new campaign for participative management, I had to instruct them. This is how you will be remunerated and so will your staff. If at the end of two years you still feel the same, we will reconsider. If at the end of the first year you don't want the bonus you have earned, I will arrange for it to go to a charity! After the first few months, the new system was quickly accepted and it is to this day the main plank of NFC's remuneration package.

Reshaping, restructuring, refinancing, remotivating, all were progressing and slowly the NFC fortunes were turning. But there were much larger political forces at play which would radically reshape our whole future.

4

The Road to Privatization

'It is a totally unique denationalization package. The daring management of the NFC is
putting together a £50m deal which will
save government the embarrassment of
offering up this rag-bag company for public
sale some time next year.'
Daily Express, 19 June 1981

'Peter Thompson is the Chief Executive of
what until recently has been perceived of
as a boring, inefficient, lame duck.'
Sunday Telegraph, 21 June 1981

In the world outside NFC, Prime Minister James Callaghan
surprisingly decided not to go for a general election in the autumn
of 1978. Instead he chose to govern into the final year of a
five-year term – always a risky political scenario. In the event,
the trade unions, the traditional allies of the Labour government,
turned on him. Unable to accept another year of wage restraints
and unable to control their members, the UK went through 'the
winter of discontent'. Month after month there were strikes in
one sector after another.

The Conservatives were ready for the election. They had
produced a manifesto in 1979 which contained a section on
privatization – 'pushing back the frontiers of state ownership'.
Bearing in mind what an important and central theme it has
been in the decade of Thatcher government, it did not have as
prominent a place in the manifesto as one might have supposed.
Considering the mighty industrial giants that have been, or are
in the process of being, privatized – British Telecom, British Gas,

British Aerospace, British Airways, Water and Electricity – it is surprising that little NFC ever got a mention.

However, privatization had small beginnings and Norman Fowler had claimed a place in the manifesto. He saw no possible reason for NFC to remain in state ownership. At the party conference in 1978 I remember him being particularly forceful, asking why a travel and household removals business should be in state ownership. He was nonetheless a realist. He did not believe that NFC could ever be viable while it was having to shoulder the losses of National Carriers. He offered to split NFC in two. The viable part would be taken to the market by way of an offer for sale on the Stock Exchange, and the unviable National Carriers would remain as a government-owned business, or possibly be returned to British Rail.

No other nationalized corporations were mentioned in the manifesto. We were the only one – alongside us were state-owned limited liability companies such as Cable & Wireless and Amersham International. When the Conservatives were elected, Norman Fowler was rather unusually appointed as Secretary of State for Transport, the department he had shadowed in opposition. With his appointment we concluded that, like it or not, by one means or another, we would be privatized (an unfortunate term to which my coarser colleagues attribute unpleasant sexual connotations).

At the first board meeting after the election, our chairman Bobbie Lawrence suggested that we should take the initiative and appoint city advisers to see whether the new government's proposals had any basis in reality. Would investors see NFC as a worthwhile punt? We chose the financial advisers that were best suited to NFC's particular needs, and arranged for five of the well-known merchant banks to make presentations to us on how they would tackle the privatization of NFC.

Before any advisers were invited to take part in the beauty parade, one issue had to be resolved. Should we take up Norman Fowler's offer – made in the irresponsible days of opposition – to split NFC into two? It would certainly allow us to shuffle off the problems of National Carriers and get rid of the losses which they were still making.

My view was that the business should be divided. I had

struggled with the problems of National Carriers for over five years. I knew that many depot closures and consequential redundancies were still necessary before it could be made viable, and that the two-union problem would not go away. I therefore voted for separation. The board, being able to take a more detached view, argued strongly that NFC should stay a single entity. First, there was the value of the properties that NFC had inherited, many of them in city centres, which belonged to National Carriers. Secondly, if we released National Carriers from our control, we would be creating a subsidized competitor who would depress the whole road transport market with subsidized pricing. Finally, if we were prepared to preside over one break-up, the politicians might be tempted to go on and sell other profitable companies in the business and leave us to manage the companies that had no market worth. As ever stubborn, I could not bring myself to agree with the board judgement but with hindsight they were right. In major issues of this kind, non-executives have a critical role to play. No board should be without them!

The merchant banks contest was won by Schroder Wragg. To save double fees and because at this stage there was no conflict of interest, the government also appointed them as their financial advisers. Schroders approached the analysis with enthusiasm and thoroughness. The verdict was that, recognizing the progress NFC had made since 1976 and assuming the trend continued, and given one or two provisos, they advised that an offer for sale of NFC on the Stock Exchange was possible. The one or two provisos amounted to a requirement that government should properly fund the pension schemes, and would have to write off most of the debt from the balance sheet. Pensions always present a problem in privatizations. In the 1970s almost all the nationalized sector under successive Labour governments agreed to inflation-proofed pensions. The decisions were really government inspired, and were taken under pressure from the trade unions, but the pension funds were not always enhanced to fulfil this obligation.

High inflation in the late 1970s with negative net rate of returns on pension fund investments also did not help. Pensions were to be a further headache when it came to the buy-out.

The process of dressing up NFC and making it ready for

sale was started. Our status had to be changed from being a state-owned corporation to being a commercial limited liability company with its own articles of association. In state ownership our articles, the rules by which we were allowed to play the commercial game, were enshrined in the act of parliament that set us up. So unless the act stipulated that we could do something, we were not legally allowed to do it. Of course it was always up to the government of the day to interpret our powers under the act as widely or narrowly as it liked. A Labour government would tend to encourage us to widen and expand our business base, whereas a Conservative government would want to constrain and restrict us.

For example, a never-ending political issue was whether we should be allowed to use our extensive network of maintenance depots to repair other people's vehicles. The Motor Agents' Association tended to resist our incursions into what they regarded as their members' field of business. Labour allowed us to expand into third party engineering; Conservatives required us to retreat.

Any half-decent lawyer will make sure that a normal company will have articles of association that allow the directors to play almost any business game they want. A company is usually required to consult with the shareholders if it wants fundamentally to change its business; but in the main directors of commercial companies can follow their entrepreneurial noses where the business scent takes them. Not true of nationalized businesses. If their acts of parliament do not specifically permit it, they cannot do it. Yet another burden to ensure mediocre performance for the industries we all own in common. We made sure that our new articles of association, while stressing that we were primarily a transport and travel company, nevertheless allowed us to do anything which was, in the opinion of the directors, beneficial to the health of the business.

So the necessary bill went through parliament, part of a wider Transport Bill dealing mainly with the deregulation of the bus industry. But even as the Bill was making its progress through the two houses, trading was getting manifestly tougher outside in the market place. The world was running into recession, and in an attempt to get inflation under control in the UK, the government had become obsessed with the concept of control of the money supply. Monetarism was the flavour of the year. Inflation, they argued, was a result of too much money and credit being created in the financial system. Curb this and inflation will come under control. Restricting credit and money supply naturally reduced demand for goods and services just at the time when the world was heading in any case for recession. As a result of this policy, while the rest of the world caught a cold, the UK was governed into catching pneumonia.

Most of NFC's business was with manufacturing industry. In the space of twelve months, while the Transport Bill was making its slow way through parliament, the volume of goods to be carried fell like a stone. Many customers were either going out of business or retrenching. The net outcome was that profits, in sympathy with volume, declined. As I said earlier, it was also the moment when the government indirectly made certain that NFC could not be taken to the stock market by taking away our largest contract.

It is hardly surprising that Hugh Ashton, who was leading the Schroder team, advised government that with falling profits, and having lost its major contract, NFC had not a hope of a successful flotation on the stock market for at least two or three years. However, before the thumbs-down was finally given, Schroders had been asked for their view of the price the government could expect to get for NFC. The problem was that the pension deficiency was so great that fully funding it might well cost more than the company could realize when it was sold. Under these circumstances it would have been politically difficult to go ahead with the flotation. Schroders' view was that in the market conditions of late 1980 the company would be worth between £50m and £55m. This would leave a comfortable surplus over the estimated cost of funding the pension deficit.

I was surprised at the value. I did believe that, with all the work we had put in to improve the business, it was worth more. But, on reflection, can you point to any chairman or chief executive who believes that the market fairly rates his business? After hearing the figure I travelled down to Aberdovey for one of the golfing weekends.

After the normal thirty-six holes of golf, and a gourmet

six-course dinner – washed down by much port and wine – the conversation turned to business! I remember saying, 'Those City slickers only value our company that we have sweated our guts over for nine years at between £50m and £55m. At that price we should raise the money and buy it ourselves!' There was general approval for this piece of jingoism, but the mood moved on to more pressing pursuits like the rendering of the classic folk song 'We are off to see the Wild West show!'

Elsewhere others, like our lawyer Philip Mayo and accountant James Watson, were having similar thoughts. So, faced with the advice that the company could not go to the market, it is hardly surprising that we began to develop the concept of a management buy-out. There had been one or two smaller management buy-outs and we wondered why this route should not be equally viable for a large business. Driven by Ted Wall, our International Director, and Jack Mather, now our Chief Executive, its appeal widened. At the same time, all my socialist instincts of yesteryear came to the fore. Why not make it an employee buy-out and include the whole of the workforce? But the company we wanted to create had to be different from a consensus cooperative which cannot take difficult decisions; different from a normal capitalistic company where the emphasis is too much upon the satisfaction of the needs of the shareholders; different from a nationalized industry where the concept of ownership in common had failed to motivate. Our 'different' company finally emerged in concept and vision as a new form of employee capitalism. The company would be owned by the employees who would *buy* rather than be given the shares. They would have a role to play in the policy-making of the business, but the managers would have the mandate to manage. All employees would share in the wealth that they created.

What was it that made the top team of NFC decide to go for an employee buy-out rather than the simpler and better trodden route of a management buy-out? Undoubtedly had we proposed a management buy-out it would have been more acceptable to the financiers. It would have been the easier route; and as management buy-outs are structured, we as individuals would have finished up with a larger share of the equity. Assuming – and this is a big assumption – the outcome was as successful, we would all now be even richer than we are today. I hope my own reasons for wanting an employee buy-out are clear from my background.

It would have been a betrayal of the values I so fervently believed in to have proposed a management buy-out. I felt sure that with a management buy-out nothing much would change for the workers on the shop floor. The old management would still be in charge, but because they had borrowed so heavily to buy the business, they would have to be more demanding and profit aggressive than they were before. These can be negatives rather than positives in the eyes of the workers.

My close colleagues, without any real persuasion, enthusiastically went down the route of employee involvement.

Ted Wall's reason was principally motivation:

> The management buy-out route was divisive, largely motivated by greed and led to the abuse of power. The employee route was preferable not only in equity but also the unity of purpose achieved would offer a greater chance of success to what was at the time a mixed bag of companies with a poor track record . . . My views were not influenced by political considerations but were based upon more than thirty years of commercial management experience which had convinced me of the need for a fresh approach to business which would recognize fully the relative importance of people and capital . . .

Jack Mather's desire for an employee buy-out lay in his family background.

> When the idea of a management buy-out was modified into a buy-out by all willing employees, I had no problems with this new concept. The opportunities and the risks, which hitherto would have been limited to a few, would be thrown open to all. My background had largely been in personnel management, trying to bridge the gaps between managers and workers. I had also had numerous discussions at home about the conflict between the owners of a business and those who manage on their behalf, and the workers whose directed efforts produced

76

the wealth. My father was a staunch trade unionist all his life and was an official of the chapel in one of the national newspapers. My father-in-law was a convenor at a large engineering factory in Trafford Park. Family get-togethers gave rise to plenty of concentrated debate and I could easily see how significant employee share ownership could help to span the divide between the two sides of industry.

James Watson's formative years were in a small family business.

At no time during the process of the purchase of National Freight Company Ltd from the government did I have a personal preference for a management buy-out to a buy-out which involved all the employees. Several factors in the past brought me to this position.

I had grown up in the environment of a small business owned by my father; interestingly, transport was involved. My father had always believed in a good relationship with his employees both in terms of incentive and communication – terms not recognized at that time – but through this I learned of the importance of employee involvement. I spent many weeks during my early years working with his employees and so learned their views and the way they responded. It was never a case of them and us.

In my more immediate past I had seen how in a nationalized industry there was little recognition of, or pride in, ownership. I felt that this could well be changed by the employees themselves having a direct capital stake in the business.

Philip Mayo was more interested in its effect on the political stability and health of the UK.

I did, and still do, share Peter's vision of a company which is a better company because it is owned substantially by the people who work in it. It may be that I came to this position from the opposite direction from him, in that I believe that the widest possible spread of effective wealth and power is the best guarantee against totalitarian regimes, whether of the left or the right. I believe that the best possible country is the one where the greatest number of people have a significant personal stake in its continuing wealth and prosperity.

So the buy-out had to include all the employees. This was the concept we took to the NFC board. Bobbie Lawrence spoke for all the non-executive Directors when he wished us well but doubted we would ever pull it off. He agreed to broach the subject with Norman Fowler, who immediately said he was interested. Bobbie Lawrence and I subsequently met him in his office at the House of Commons. This was an absolutely critical meeting and I had carefully prepared each point I wanted to make.

I suppose I had expected much grander surroundings in which to make the most important sales pitch in my life. We were greeted by one of the Secretary of State's aides in the entrance lobby of the House. We were taken down seemingly endless oak-panelled corridors to what really was a very modest little room. Clearly the shortage of office space in the Palace of Westminster meant that Secretaries of State could not take the spacious elegance of their offices in their Whitehall ministries with them into Parliament. As I spoke I tried to convey a message to Norman Fowler of vision, political excitement, but, above all, of confidence of achievement. What we also desperately needed was time during which he would be committed not to consider other bids or other possible means of sale of NFC, while we put in place the necessary financial and legal agreements to pull off the deal.

Norman Fowler was enthusiastic from the beginning. He saw advantages on many levels. Politically it would be one of the first privatizations of a state corporation to which he was committed by manifesto. The way we proposed to do it would, if successful, solve one of the great problems of UK Ltd – the endless industrial class struggle which had resulted in the British sickness of strikes and disruption of production. It would also give the Conservatives the credit for facilitating a form of worker involvement and ownership which Labour had talked about but had never really been able to deliver. It would be stealing their political clothes –

and few politicians can resist this opportunity. On another level Fowler saw that if the company could make a success of the participative and sharing values that would result from employee ownership, it would be a good example of a different and less harsh form of Conservative capitalism.

He wished to help but at the same time he could not risk a political or commercial fiasco, so he needed to be assured that we had City support for the financing. He and his officials needed to be satisfied that the chance of failure was small – because if it did fail, the political capital that could be made out of it by the opposition would have been more than embarrassing. Finally, he had to be able to justify his actions in terms of public account- ability, i.e., that he had obtained a fair price for the state assets he was selling. He asked us to come back when we had sorted out as many of these unknowns as possible.

We turned immediately to our merchant bank, Schroders, and explained the scheme to them, but after much deliberation they concluded that it was not viable and they would be unable to raise City money.

It was now that James Watson, the City-orientated Finance Director, played his key card. He explained to the rest of us financial innocents that we had gone to 'the wrong shop'. If we wanted to keep all the equity but raise the wind to buy the company mainly by borrowings, then we had to go to a merchant bank that was backed by a major lending bank.

That was how we found ourselves one Friday evening in February 1981 at No. 15/16 Gracechurch Street, the head- quarters of Barclays Merchant Bank. It was perhaps fate that the bank had as its Chief Executive the youthful but far-seeing Lord Camoys.

To this day I am surprised that he did not throw us out. Our proposal was that collectively the workforce might be able to raise £5m. We needed about £57m to buy the company and we needed perhaps another £40m of credit lines to finance the business once we had bought it. We wanted Barclays to lend us the money on reasonable commercial terms, but we needed to keep all the equity – for if this was to be a true employee company it had to be owned completely by the employees! What went through Tom Camoys's mind I can't imagine, but he did manage to keep a straight face. Having heard us courteously, and having asked a number of penetrating banker questions – for example, had we enough earnings to pay the interest on the borrowings? – the innovative possibilities of the proposal must have inspired him. He asked for an adjournment and he retired from the room with his colleagues. When he came back he told us that, while there could be no certainty that he would support us, he would put in his best team from the merchant bank to evaluate our proposals. He hoped the scheme was feasible. The team would be led by his Deputy Managing Director, Ron Watson, who was a lending banker, and had been put into the merchant bank to provide a bridge between the newly emerging merchant bank and the lending bank. We were to learn what a fine man he was: pragmatic, full of common sense and prepared to take a risk providing he rated the people to whom he was lending. We fixed for the team to visit our headquarters in Bedford the following Wednesday.

Rarely have I known our team prepare so thoroughly for any meeting. Many years afterwards Ron Watson told me that when his team assembled at St Pancras to travel up on the train to Bedford, the general view was that they were wasting their time. They had had over the weekend an opportunity of seeing the financials we had prepared, and in banking terms they really did not stack up. By the time they returned to London that evening, we had managed to persuade them that it was worth working with us to see if we could make banking and financial sense of the employee buy-out.

The presentation followed its usual course. I started off with the history of the business and the vision of where it might go. Mike Sweet, our planner, a sound and sane Yorkshireman from Hull, took them through the corporate plan for the next three years. James Watson, with whom the bank representatives all felt comfortable as a kindred spirit, presented the financials. Philip Mayo, the lawyer, followed, giving them a flavour of the principles that we had to hold on to if the deal was to go forward. In essence, we had to buy the whole company; the employees and pensioners had to have the major stake of the equity; no one should be compelled to buy or sell his shares; share ownership could not be a condition of employment; and some kind of mechanism would be established to allow employees to deal in the shares. I rounded off with the vision of what could be achieved in a labour-intensive service industry if only we could get rid of the 'us and them' – management and labour – attitude and how that could happen if we were all owners of our company, NFC, pulling in the same direction.

We adjourned for lunch, and over lunch we let the Group Managing Directors have a go at the banking team by taking them through their own parts of the business – warts and all.

It was Ron Watson's turn to do the questioning. I waited with my head full of asset values, gearing, interest cover – all subjects that the team had boned up on over the previous three days. To my amazement, he first wanted to know how we trained our people. For a full hour the questioning went on and on about the strength of management, labour relations, motivational concepts, participative management style – people, people, people. I was amazed and impressed. I knew the strength of NFC was its employees. I was surprised to find that bankers knew it too.

We did get round to the assets eventually. We were able to tempt them with the potential values of our inner city sites, particularly of National Carriers – although, in all honesty, during the depression of 1981 no one realized how valuable they were to become in the boom years of the late 1980s.

What changed the team's views? Here is Ron Watson's account:

> The BMB team arrived at the meeting on Wednesday, 29 April, feeling that the chances of success were slim, maybe ten to one against. However, the odds shortened dramatically by late afternoon.
>
> During the morning session NFC board members gave a highly professional presentation of the business. They were obviously very competent communicators which would be of crucial importance when the time came to approach employees to buy shares. It was also encouraging that while current profits were poor and the economy in recession, future prospects seemed brighter and cash flow was satisfactory.
>
> NFC was property rich and the team could turn their

minds to the possibility of asset backing for the banking package. The prime need was to ease bankers' minds as to the degree of risk thereby persuading them to accept a more modest equity share so achieving employee control. While the team felt that a secured banking package was vital, staring them in the face was the dreaded section 54 of the Companies Act. [This made it illegal to borrow money to buy a company and to pledge the assets of that company as collateral for the loan.]

Perhaps the key feature of the whole day was the enthusiasm of the Chief Executive and his colleagues. It was infectious; they were determined to succeed and prepared to back their words with some cash, probably borrowed. Later that day a plan of action was agreed, and the team left feeling that the odds had dropped to around three to one against. The team was equally committed to success but were of the opinion that Peter Thompson underestimated section 54, whereas they knew it could be compared in legal terms with the north face of the Eiger.

Over the next six weeks there were many meetings with the banking team. They wanted to see other levels of our management. They inspected the key premises. They evaluated the strategies. They researched with our help the markets in which we operated. Finally Ron Watson phoned to say that in principle Barclays Merchant Bank were prepared to lend us £55m to buy the company and provide a further £70m facility for working capital *subject to documentation*. It was an innocent-enough phrase but full of boulders against each of which we could stub our toes.

There was one further step to take before we could go back to the Secretary of State and make the initiative public. I had to be sure that I had the enthusiastic support of the top one hundred managers in the business. Without their commitment to the scheme itself – they would have to be prepared to sell it to their subordinates and to invest their own money – we could not launch.

However, before this there had been a touching little scene in the board room at Bedford. The bankers' support was conditional upon the 'gang of ten' senior directors being prepared to commit themselves to investing an average of £25,000 of their own money. Banks are *not* philanthropists. They judged that if the whole venture was a failure, it had to hurt us as much as it would hurt them. I think they got the relativity wrong. I had decided to invest £40,000 – I judged this to be the amount which I could reasonably risk.

If it all went wrong, I would have to sell my house but I would still have had enough left after repaying the loan to buy a smaller house. I didn't feel it was right to leave my family without an abode if my speculation was wrong. If I had lost my stake of £40,000, it would have been a sight more painful to me and my family than to Barclays if they had lost some £100m! Any self-respecting bank loses more than that a month lending to the Third World!

The ceremony was straightforward. I addressed them. 'Up to now we have all been enthused by a great new concept. The concept will not get off the ground unless the people around this table are prepared to commit themselves to pledge an average of £25,000 each. I do not wish to embarrass anyone, but I'd like you each to write on a slip of paper the amount you would be prepared to commit. Pass this forward to Philip Mayo, and he will then tell us whether we have the necessary financial as well as conceptual backing.'

Everyone wrote down a figure and passed their slips to Philip and he retired. He returned within five minutes (which was something of a miracle because lawyers are notoriously slow at arithmetic) and announced that the minimum average commitment was well exceeded.

This was an important first step. If we as leaders were not prepared to give a commitment by second mortgaging our homes, or to charge them as collateral against our loans, the buy-out could not have progressed. It sent forth a great message that we collectively were prepared to put our money where our mouths were.

We called the top one hundred managers to Bedford. We decided it was such an important decision for them to take that they should be able to reflect on their decision overnight. We spent two and a half hours talking to them about the scheme.

We had Michael Peterson, the merchant banker, with us, and we were also supported by Peter Tyley, the local director of National Westminster Bank. An important consideration for anyone when making the decision as to how much to invest would be the terms on which personal loans could be obtained from the bank. Barclays were leading on the corporate lending, NatWest enthusiastically agreed to lead on personal lending.

Following the presentation there were a number of immediate questions. By about 6 p.m. we asked them all to go back to their hotels. We had arranged for them to have dinner with their own *company* colleagues. So all the BRS management were together, similarly the Pickfords team, National Carriers, and so on. The main board directors visited one or more of the groups during the evening to solicit reactions and to answer questions.

The group I visited was Pickfords. Another colleague went to BRS. Around the BRS dinner table he found nothing but enthusiasm for the concept. They knew they wanted to be involved; their problem was how much they should each invest and how likely the scheme was to be successful. The enthusiasm was understandable because they knew well most of the key members of the buy-out team. The restructured senior management of NFC, following the major losses in 1975, had come about entirely from BRS. They trusted us and had confidence that NFC could be made successful.

When I joined the Pickfords group of senior management I found a very different atmosphere. Pickfords had always been proudly independent. They had never enjoyed their ownership by NFC. They had in the past gone out of their way to minimize the connection between Pickfords and the NFC. The mood of the meeting when I joined it was pessimistic. If we had been asking them to invest their money directly into Pickfords, then they had no problems. If Pickfords could be bought from NFC by the Pickfords management, they would organize such a buy-out. But to ask them to put their money into NFC, a business they did not admire and whose results over the years had caused them personal and customer embarrassment, was too much. One manager went so far as to say that we, the NFC team, were seeking their financial involvement to bale out a bankrupt business.

I answered the points they were making as well as I could. I made it clear that a separate buy-out and investment in Pickfords was *not* on the agenda. We were offering them the only game in town. After an hour and a half of pretty negative debate, I stood up and with some anger left the room saying, 'You please yourselves, but I intend to retire from NFC a millionaire.' Instinctively I felt the vision of an employee-owned business was not what would win the day, so I appealed to their pockets and, I suppose, their greed. But also as I left I vowed that one day I would make them as proud of being part of NFC as they were of being Pickfords.

Although I was angry when I left, I did understand their feelings. It also made me recognize what a difficult communication task we were facing when we came to persuade the workforce in general to part with their money and to invest in NFC. The first interest of the employee was his own depot; next, he was aware of the company that he worked for (e.g., BRS or Pickfords), but even this was a little remote. Now we were asking him to put his money into NFC which bought and sold nothing, employed only a few people at headquarters, had no trucks, depots or shops in its livery and had only come into existence some eleven years before as a result of a political decision. This would make the task of capturing the attention, imagination and enthusiasm of the workforce even more difficult. I should have recognized it earlier, and perhaps I had, but I had put it to the back of my mind. Either way, the attitude of the Pickford senior management that evening brought it right to the forefront. It was yet another hurdle we had to jump which was potentially higher than I had recognized.

Geoff Pygall was the forthright, irascible, emotional but much respected Group Managing Director of Pickfords, which he had joined as a boy of fifteen, some forty years earlier. He had the responsibility of pulling together the Pickford senior management, and reporting back the following day on where they stood. In the event he was able to report 100 per cent support, and the clear intention of each of them to invest at least the required amount per head. He did tell me that my millionaire's exit line had captured their attention, and from then on the tide swayed in favour of the buy-out!

The following day we had gathered 99 per cent support for the scheme from the key group of senior managers. They were prepared to invest to the level required and, more importantly, they were prepared to sell the concept to their own employees. If the workforce were to be convinced we needed all the management as salesmen. The message could not be put over to a 23,000 workforce in 1100 different locations by only the top ten directors.

We now had the commitment of the bank, and we had the commitment of the one hundred managers. We were ready to announce the deal to the world at large, providing the political will was there.

Much work had been going on to earn the necessary political support. There were two key players – Sir Robert Lawrence, our Chairman, at the official level, and Frank Law, one of our long-serving non-executive directors, on the equally important but less well-understood unofficial network.

Frank Law is an unusual man. He was born in Germany and had come to the UK in the 1930s to escape the persecution of the Jews under Hitler. He adopted the UK as his own country. He was in intelligence during the war, and eventually developed a commercial career in the UK. He moved in political circles with always left-of-centre instincts. Today he is one of the few staunch supporters of David Owen and the SDP. One thing we have shared in common from the beginning is the belief in industrial democracy. We were happy to build it together in the NFC. He knew all the key political players socially, and had been appointed a non-executive director of NFC by Richard Marsh when it was set up in 1968. He witnessed the highs and lows of NFC's fortunes throughout the 1970s. However, he really came into his own when the buy-out was advanced. He knew Norman Fowler well and later became godfather to his daughter. He mixed with the key civil servants and was trusted and respected by them. He was not averse to writing to the Prime Minister if he felt this would help the buy-out along. He oiled the wheels, he encouraged us all when it looked as if we were not going to find a way through, but, above all, as a great friend he was able to advise caution and indeed threaten me if I became impossible and unreasonable in my determination to get my own way on everything! So we had one supporter beavering away on our behalf below the official surface.

Bobbie Lawrence, as the official liaison between us and the government, had to hold a balance between the interests of the existing owners of the business – the government – and the would-be owners – the employees led by the senior management.

Although we needed it, we did not ask for the inside track. It was something which could have been difficult for any minister to grant. But we felt that, as long as we continued to make progress, and that the price we were offering could be shown to be fair by impartial city advisers, Norman Fowler would give us the necessary time to put together a scheme. We thought the time we needed was six months, in the event it took nearly twelve.

To make progress we had to have the proposals made public as soon as possible so we could have the key decision takers openly committed to its success. With political, banking and top management support, there would now be nothing to stop the announcement to the media and nothing to stop Norman Fowler telling Parliament.

It was time to take stock of what was driving the management. Three strong motivations were at play: fear, greed and vision.

Fear: if we did not buy the company the only alternative open to the government, not being able to take it to the stock market, would be to put NFC up for auction, either whole (as, for example, Sealink) or in parts (as, for example, the National Bus Company). New owners would then take over and they might have very different ideas about how to develop the company. As so often happens in takeovers, this would mean that the top management would be fired and there would be massive restructuring further down the business.

Greed: I suspect we all felt that if we could make a success of it we might take a few bob from our investment. Nobody imagined in his wildest dream how much that would be.

Vision: looking back on all the debates and discussions, I know that this was the dominant motivation. The thought of presiding over a business whose culture would be about participation, involvement, and sharing with the employees the wealth that these values would create, was what excited most of the team.

5

The Deal is Fixed

'500 staff meetings, 30 lawyers, 25 Civil
Servants, 6 management briefings, 3 QCs, 2
Secretaries of State, one Act of Parliament
– four months later I had come to realize it
wasn't quite as simple as I thought.'
SIR PETER THOMPSON, 19 October 1981

'If the failure of British industry in recent
years has been the failure of management
to manage and workers to work, the NFC
cheerfully expects to cure both maladies in
one fell swoop.'
The Times, 22 February 1982

The problems came out of the woodwork almost as soon as the
announcements were made. The first, the one that caused the
most delay, and almost proved to be the reef on which the deal
sank, was how we were to give security to the bankers for the
loan. The only security we had was the assets of the company
we were seeking to buy. Company law at the time would not
allow a predator wishing to take over a company to pledge the
assets of the company as security. Although I hadn't looked upon
us as such, we – the senior managers – were predators in the
eyes of the law. Section 54 of the Companies Act says, 'Thou
shalt not pledge the assets of the company you are seeking to
buy in order to raise the money to buy it.'

In most circumstances this law was sensible, as it provided
protection to the existing creditors of a company against the
behaviour of an unreasonable predator. The reasoning was fair.
On the strength of the balance sheet someone may have given

credit to, or lent money to, a company believing that he was lending to a company of substance. If things went wrong and the company went bankrupt, creditors were entitled, provided the funds existed, to receive their money back from the liquidator in a certain order of priority. The preferred creditors, such as bank loans secured against the assets of the business, came first; the employees got their entitlement to outstanding wages next; and the normal trade creditors were third in line. It was clearly not fair for the potential new owners of the business, simply because they needed to borrow money to buy the company, to put a new set of lenders – i.e. the banking syndicate who were lending the money to buy the company – in front of the existing creditors. The existing creditors would find themselves further down the queue for payment if things went wrong and they were thus prejudiced. Company law was clear that, never mind the worthiness of the predators, the existing creditors had to be protected.

When Barclays stood alongside us they thought the way ahead for them to lend the money fully secured was simple. The vast majority of the loan price would be used by the company to pay off the deficiencies of the pension scheme. These deficiencies had arisen in the 1970s. As I explained, almost all the nationalized industries, encouraged by the trade unions who were supported in turn by the Labour government, granted inflation-proofed pensions to their employees. This very desirable benefit was never properly funded. The government had not required the nationalized industries to provide the cash to top up the portfolios of investments that the pension funds needed in order to take on the additional pension obligations. The understanding was that when and if the pension funds were unable to pay out the promised pensions, the government would be there to make up the shortages. As we were casting adrift from government, our pension trustees said they wanted the money now, and were not satisfied with a vague promise that it would be available later.

In the event, at least £48.7m of the £53.5m eventual purchase price was used for this purpose by the government. The pension funds were considered to be the highest preferred creditors, and would rank above all other creditors. Therefore, all that had to happen was that the banks – by lending the company the money to repay the pension deficiency – could slip into the place of the pension scheme and become the preferred creditor themselves. In other words, by paying off the man in the front of the credit queue you could take his place.

This proposal was put to Richard Sykes, the QC most respected in City circles for his views on company law. I have never met Mr Sykes, but his judgments on which I so often waited with bated breath meant the difference between happiness or despair for all of twelve months. I understand from Philip Mayo, who, together with our lawyers, was in constant touch with him, that he was on our side but it seemed as if the law was not. The opinion emerged that the pension fund could not be regarded as a preferred creditor as it was the government and not NFC who really owed the pension fund the money to make up the deficit. It was back to the drawing board.

Perhaps the government could be persuaded to require us by law to fund in full the pension fund deficit? Obligations taken on as a result of being *legally* required to do so would have priority status without causing legal problems from the existing creditors. We attended yet another meeting with the ministry – four of us, the usual twelve of them. We would have always been outnumbered if it had ever come to a vote. Civil servants do seem to hunt in large packs. Trying to help on the government's side was the then Junior Minister Kenneth Clarke, who subsequently has had such a distinguished political career, latterly taking on the awesome task of trying to bring management and value for money into the National Health Service. He was a lawyer by training. He quickly recognized that, under the powers granted to the Minister under the Transport Act, he had the necessary legal authority to issue a statutory instrument, which has the force of law, by which the company was required fully to fund its own pension fund. However, he felt that the powers to issue the statutory instrument had been given by Parliament with other purposes in mind. It could be an abuse of power to use it in these special circumstances, even though he was as anxious as the next man to see NFC privatized by way of the employee buy-out.

He decided we should refer the matter to the Attorney-

General, the highest legal authority outside the House of Lords. It took some time, as indeed all these issues did. The judgment, when it came, was that the Minister certainly had the power to make the statutory instrument but it would be an inappropriate use of ministerial powers so to do. Yet again we had reached a dead end.

The banking team, however, had become so enthused by the whole concept, and the NFC team and the professional advisers had built up such strong relationships over the months, that no one wanted to see the deal founder on a legal technicality. There *was* a way forward and that was for Barclays to lend unsecured! In the event of failure, though, they would not have prior claim over the other creditors if the assets had to be sold. Ron Watson decided to put the case for an unsecured loan to the senior general manager of the lending bank, John Quinton. He had already had a distinguished career with Barclays, and he was subsequently to become the first individual who was not from one of the founding families to become Chairman of the whole group. He took what was for us a momentous decision. Rather than see the initiative founder, he *would* be prepared to lend unsecured. He would also commit Barclays to lend the whole amount if the other banks, who had been approached to join the loan syndicate, would not accept similar terms. Banks are frequently criticized for their unwillingness to support innovation. They cannot be accused of this in our case.

Of course, they wanted their commercial pound of flesh. At the stage in the negotiations we had reached, we had agreed that the syndicate of banks should have 'as an equity sweetener' 15 per cent of the share capital. This left the employees and families with 85 per cent. If Barclays had to lend unsecured, they demanded, in return for the extra risk involved, 40 per cent of the equity. The price was high but rather than abort the deal it was one we would have been willing to pay. In addition, a complex system was devised which would enable Barclays through time – as existing loans and creditors were paid off – to get their loans back to where they wanted them to be – first in line behind the assets.

But at times luck does favour the bold. We learnt in the late summer of 1981 that there was a new Company Bill going through Parliament which, if all went well, could be on the statute book and hence law by the late autumn. The government was seeking to open the way to encourage management buy-outs. There was a section in the Bill designed to subordinate existing creditors to new borrowings where a management buy-out was proposed. We concluded that, with the addition of the odd phrase of clarification, the 1981 Act could be our route through – we could still hang on to 85 per cent of the equity.

Now we had a decision to take. It was nearly six months since the announcement was made in February. We had said to the staff, the media and the business community that the employees would be the new owners within six months. The delays and setbacks meant it was getting more and more difficult to sustain the interest of the staff. Yet to wait for the new Act of Parliament would certainly mean that the deal could not be completed until February 1982 – a full twelve months after the announcement. The decision we made was that the extra 25 per cent of the shares being retained by the employees was worth the delay.

The legal Grand National was finally completed in November. The new Companies Act was law. In constant consultation with Richard Sykes we designed the necessary legal format to make use of the appropriate section of the Act. In essence it required every director of any subsidiary board in the NFC (and there were over sixty such boards) to make a solemn declaration that the takeover of the NFC by the new company, and the consequent borrowing of the £57m to purchase the company, would *not* in the opinion of each of those directors weaken the commercial strength and prospects of the NFC. It required great faith on behalf of all those directors to make that declaration, but as they were willing to do it, it gave me added comfort that the senior management of NFC were still 100 per cent behind the new form of company.

I have given you a résumé of many thousand legal hours of debate. It is probably the only major buy-out in history where the legal fees were greater than the merchant-banking fees. (In fairness to the firms of lawyers involved, their charges were also discounted.)

But the legal problems were not our only problems. One issue that simply would not go away in the early months was the question of who would pay for the costs that were being clocked up if the whole exercise failed. The merchant bank were advising us on the basis of no success, no fee. But no such arrangement existed with the lawyers and accountants. We were also incurring costs in communicating with the staff. The final bill for communications and advice added up to more than £1.5m. We argued that we were acting as agents for the Secretary of State for Transport. He had given us his blessing. This was *his* preferred route for privatization. Therefore, if it did not succeed, he, or more probably the NFC, should pick up the bill. The civil servants never accepted this argument. Indeed they were very anxious to know, for example, who paid for the dinner and the night's accommodation for the one hundred managers when we brought them together to see if we had their support. We were always slow to answer these questions, but in that case we were able to argue that it was a normal management conference at which other issues were also discussed.

However, the questioning went on intermittently, and by July it was becoming a matter of concern to the buy-out team. Eventually it was decided that all expenditure incurred would be absorbed by the New Limited Liability Company set up to take over the NFC. In the early life of this company each of the Directors would have one share of £1, the balance of the equity and the borrowings would be guaranteed by Barclays Merchant Bank. This was another load off our minds as we sought to achieve the successful takeover. If it had gone wrong it would have cost each of us just £1. But the real cost, of course, was to our reputations. It would have cost BMB considerably more.

There was also the constant worry about accountability. It was, after all, a public asset that was being sold. The accounting officer at the Department of Transport, and behind him the Treasury, needed to be satisfied that the price being offered was fair. The way to test this was, of course, to offer the company for sale to other buyers. If this route was followed, it would have ended the employee buy-out. The complications we had to overcome in pioneering employee ownership meant we needed time. An auction of a company does not allow that time.

The argument that we advanced, which was accepted by the

politicians, but with less enthusiasm by the Treasury, was that their merchant bank had advised them in 1980 that the company was not financially strong enough to be floated on the Stock Exchange. If it achieved its corporate plan, which demanded ambitious profit improvement, it would be worth about £55m in three years' time. We were offering around that sum two years earlier. In addition, we were prepared to buy the company without demanding any warranties from the seller. When any company is bought, the buyer requires the seller to stand behind the financial statements that are made as the basis of the sale. For example, if the seller says the assets are worth a certain amount and in the event they are shown not to be, the buyer can seek commercial or legal recompense from the seller. We asked as buyers for no such warranties. We said to the government, we know the company, we will buy it — warts and all. After all, if anyone knew its strengths and weaknesses we did.

But government was reluctant to make a decision on the price until everything else was in place. We needed to know whether we could afford it from the beginning. Some kind of understanding developed which was never formalized until late October that the price would be between £50m and £55m. Representing the buyers, I never had any face-to-face negotiations with the government — the seller. It was done between the merchant banks. When everything else was settled except the price, I had to concede via Barclays an extra £1m to Schroder Wragg to clinch the deal! Unlike any other commercial deal I have ever done, the purchase price was the last consideration — not, as usual, the first!

With the knowledge of hindsight many have said that at a price of £53.5m we stole the company. It did not seem so at the time. If we were robbers how was it that the government's advisers did not think that the City wanted to have any part in the robbery? In 1981 the industrial world was in recession and company values on the Stock Exchange were depressed. I asked for a list of companies whose asset values were more than twice their market value. The list was as long as your arm and contained many well-known businesses. Assets were not what excited the stock market in 1981. Earnings were a more appropriate measure then, as they are today. People invest in companies because of their actual and potential profitability, and their corresponding ability to pay dividends. In the preceding twelve months in public ownership the NFC had not made enough profits to pay the interest charge on the money that it had to borrow. We bought the company at a much higher price–earnings ratio than that at which its major competitor, Transport Development Group, was trading on the stock market at the time. Indeed, Sir James Duncan, their Chairman, said publicly that he would not consider buying NFC at almost any price! The fact was that NFC had to be improved for it to be worth the price we paid the government for it. In reality, we were buying our own improvements.

Although the government was naturally concerned that the price was fair, this never subsequently became a political issue; unlike a number of the other privatizations when the shares have been offered for sale on the stock market. The price fixed by the issuing house in conjunction with the brokers has several times been the subject of select committee comment, particularly when the issue has been massively oversubscribed and, once dealings have started, the price has soared. An offer for sale to the public should be a better way of ensuring a fair price to government. In practice it has been as inexact as any other method.

Another worry was that, since there were no established custom and legal practices for employee buy-outs, we found ourselves constantly innovating and improvising.

For example, a never-ending serial was the writing of the prospectus which we had to issue to employees to persuade them to invest. There was a format: a use of words well established through the courts in which prospectuses should be couched. Unfortunately, these hallowed phrases meant little to the lorry driver in Scunthorpe. We had constant debate on the issue with our lawyers.

In the end both sides compromised and divided the prospectus into two parts. Part 1 was full of drawings, photographs and exhortation, which we believed our employees would understand. Part 2 contained the legalistic and accounting jargon acceptable to the lawyers. I always felt that 'our' part was probably read more than 'their' part.

The prospectus went to 49 drafts before it was finalized, which must have been something of a record. It was all very frustrating. I argued forcibly that no prospectus was necessary. We were offering shares only to people who knew the company well – they were either working for it now, or had done so during their working lives. This view was dismissed as improper. The team just had to get down to the endless sessions, which consisted of weighing every word, checking and verifying every statement. My frustration boiled over when I was asked to verify the statement, 'I believe that employee ownership will help to eliminate the us and them of management and workers.' How can one verify a belief? All I could suggest was that I swore an affidavit. The lawyers, of course, wanted proof that if you do believe something it is a belief that it is reasonable to hold.

Isn't all this really crass nonsense supposedly to protect innocent investors? It is precisely what an individual believes that makes people want to follow him. How can one prove it is reasonable to hold a belief in a new concept? At the end of the day, I know that most people invested not on the basis of what was said in the prospectus. Prospectuses are for City people talking to City people. Our people invested because they believed in the concept, they trusted the leadership and they wanted to see their company remaining intact – rather than being sold off into unknown hands. But this was not the stuff of which normal investor documents are made, it was the stuff from which an employee buy-out is created.

I realized it was no good letting frustration get the better of me – it would not advance the cause. We had to go through the City routines even though we knew that if we were to succeed we had to reach the hearts and minds of our workforce. This needed a communication and leadership exercise of a kind which we had never before attempted.

Being a nationalized business inside which the trade union role was so dominant, we had in the past tended to communicate to our own staff through the formalized trade union machinery. We had a model consultation system, which had been negotiated and agreed with the trade unions, as long ago as 1947 when the long-distance road haulage industry was nationalized. We had local or depot consultative committees, company committees and a national committee. The trade union officials were represented at all levels if they wished to be. At local level it was usually the elected shop stewards who attended the meetings. Messages and policies were passed up and down this network. Deep down we knew it was not an effective way of communicating with our staff. After all, some of the management messages in periods of retrenchment were not very palatable. What shop steward really wanted to put over to his work mates a balanced message in these circumstances? For the buy-out we knew that management had to communicate face to face with our employees.

The decision as to how to communicate was made easier by the reaction to the news of the buy-out from our major union, the Transport & General Workers'. Following the announcement in parliament we called in representatives from all our unions to tell them of our plans. Naturally we hoped that they would welcome what we were proposing. An employee buy-out was surely better than an offer for sale on the stock market. It was surely better than putting the NFC, in whole or part, up for auction. Of course, it wasn't as acceptable to the trade unions as the company staying in public ownership, but surely they had by this time recognized that the NFC was going to be privatized, and that they had only to consider which was the better option.

In the event three of the four unions, with varying degrees of enthusiasm, accepted the buy-out as the best way forward. TSSA*, one of the three, felt it was being helpful when it declared in its union journal that an employee buy-out was, of all the options, the best way forward, but it had to remind its membership that the policy of the union was to renationalize NFC without compensation to any shareholders if a Labour government was returned to power. With support like this, who needed opposition? It surprised them when afterwards I said they had not done *too* much to help our share-selling campaign.

The problem was the TGWU. They were in conference in Brighton when we made the announcement. We despatched Jack Mather, who over the years had had many dealings with

* Transport Salaried Staff Association

97

the union, and in particular had struck up a good working relationship with Alex Kitson, its Assistant General Secretary. Kitson had always had great influence in the Commercial Drivers section of the union. He was the leader of the old Scottish Horse & Motormen's Union when it was amalgamated with the TGWU. He told many good stories of the old days of horse transportation, and claimed that when he was driving a milk delivery dray in Glasgow, he had Sean Connery as his van boy. At one conference, he cited this as an example of how two men had started at the bottom. One had become an international film star, the other working on the same horse and dray had become the Secretary of the Labour Party and number two in the most powerful union in the world. A voice interrupted from the back of the hall. 'Go on, Alex, finish the tale, tell us that the horse went on to win the Derby!'

Jack Mather and Alex Kitson had a long and affable discussion and he reported back that he believed that the TGWU would at worst take a neutral stance. He believed the union would take the view that, though they were opposed to privatization, as it was inevitable in the case of NFC they would acknowledge that the employee buy-out was the best way forward. Indeed, the first press statement made by Alex Kitson took this line. However, either his initial views were overthrown by the policy committee or he changed his mind. Perhaps what finally decided him lay in the remark he made to Jack Mather as he left: 'If this goes through it will be harder to get the lads through the gate, Jack.' Whatever the reason, the outcome was that NFC's largest union decided to oppose the buy-out and to campaign against it.

They issued a pamphlet which contained the following:

> *Why the answer should be no*
> This Union exists to preserve, protect and promote the interests of members. On that basis we are advising you not to buy shares in the National Freight Company.
> What happens?
>
> – to collective bargaining and Union organization in this proposed new set up of worker shareholders? There could be serious conflict of interest and damaging division of loyalties . . .

Workers' strength lies in unity and unity is not fostered
by divided loyalties.

In effect they were saying that in the past they had won the best
possible deal from the company by their members being united
against the management. If they owned shares they might be concerned about the value of their share stake and confused about
whether to oppose management. They might even become less
loyal to the union. If this happened, the winning of wage and
employment improvements would be at risk. Worse still, they
might become more loyal to their company than to their union.

A depressing analysis, but much of the malaise of British
industry in the 1960s and 1970s stemmed from this fundamental
tenet of trade unionism. The union is more important than the
company. In Japan the reverse is the case – maybe this is a result
less of union weakness than of Japanese management skill and
resolve to capture the hearts and minds of their own employees.
It is something that British industry is at last learning.

So we had to persuade our employees to invest over the heads
of the major union. I remember appearing with Alex Kitson on
'Newsnight', the BBC current affairs programme. He was making
the point that it was not a cooperative we were seeking to
establish: the workers would have little say in the running of
the business, the employees would lose their money, the buy-out
would be paid for by redundancies in the workforce. I did my
best to counter these arguments by presenting a vision of a
united workforce, with everyone sharing in the wealth they
were collectively creating. Hugh Scully, the interviewer, asked
me the final question: 'How can you justify encouraging your
workers to put their money into a risky venture in which they
might "lose their shirt"?' My response was simple.

'I don't expect them to lose their shirts, although of course
this could happen. I just want them to have the chance of getting
a new suit.' At my son's school where the sixth form were
watching the interview, I was from then on known as 'new-suit
Thompson'.

Undoubtedly it was the attitude of the TGWU which resulted
in less than half of our employees initially investing. It was a
very difficult time in 1981 for a working man to go against the

views of his union, but there were many examples of workers going against the grain.

One such case was in Birmingham. A meeting was held by a local director, Alan Macpherson, as part of the communication exercise to present the buy-out proposals face to face to all our employees. He is a down-to-earth Scot who was totally supportive of the buy-out. Just before the meeting started, the local shop steward, Alfie Hull, walked in with his wife and sat at the front of the meeting. Alan Macpherson's spirits sagged. Nevertheless, he made the presentation, showed the specially prepared video and invited questions. The first man on his feet was Alfie Hull. He made it clear that he was representing the official view of the TGWU. His union was implacably opposed to the privatization of the NFC; they were against any form of investment by their members in NFC. That was union policy, that was also the policy of Branch No. 5/35M. 'But as for me,' he pronounced, 'I can recognize a good deal when I see one, and I and my wife are going to invest as much as we can afford and we wish the buy-out all success.' Up and down the country individual employees were saying to their union, 'You advise us on industrial relations, but don't tell us how to spend our own money. Don't instruct us to turn down this unique form of employee capitalism.'

The TGWU's opposition to the buy-out meant that we had to devise a communications programme which was even more intense than we had originally planned. It was even more crucial now to reach every member of our workforce. We had to ensure that they were receiving not just a single message from a single source, but communication on a regular basis until the buy-out was complete, and from as many sources as possible – pamphlets, company magazines, newspapers, radio and, above all, the television. We recognized that, even more important than the management telling them it was a good thing to invest, it was vital that they read and heard it was a good thing from media commentators. The 'bounce off the wall' process, as media analysts call it, by which neighbours talk favourably about the deal was of the utmost importance.

We set about analysing our audience. In the main we would be addressing people who had never before held any shares.

This was long before the days of the growth of popular share ownership brought about by the major promotional campaigns which preceded the privatization of British Gas and British Telecom, for example. In 1981 less than one family in ten had ever held any shares. Share ownership was almost a class issue – the bosses might be interested in the stock market, the workers certainly were not. So we had to educate. The initial video we produced set out to describe exactly what a share in a company was all about. It entitled you to dividends, to voting rights and ultimately to the control of the company. We explained that any public company was actually owned by its shareholders. It was fundamental stuff, but our research showed that because before now they thought they had no reason to, not all our employees understood these fundamentals. The potential shareholder had to have the basic knowledge of share ownership before we went on to deliver the more complicated message: the vision we had for the company; how we hoped to get rid of the historic conflict of 'us and them'; how we would take the important policy decisions of the business together; how we would trade shares because we had given an undertaking to the politicians not to seek a quotation on the stock market for at least five years; how we needed some kind of internal dealing system; how employees could raise money; what our dividend policy would be (in the early years it was a strange one – to attempt to pay by way of dividends enough to cover the interest that employees and pensioners would be paying if they needed to borrow to buy the shares); how we could not guarantee anyone a job simply because they invested – increased employment opportunities could only come from success and growth, and we could not guarantee this either.

The messages were many and complex. We knew we could not communicate them without the help not only of the top hundred managers but also of the next two thousand managers. They had to be our ambassadors and salesmen. It is doubtful whether we could have promoted the sales campaign in this way today because of the investor protection legislation which now makes it illegal for anyone other than a registered independent adviser to offer investment advice!

The first act of communication was to ensure that on the day we announced the buy-out every employee had in his hand before he left work a pamphlet giving him the broad outline of what was proposed. We did not want him to read about it in the newspapers or see it on the television first. The pamphlet also advised that they would be hearing more details about the scheme at their workplaces.

The following week we addressed the two thousand managers in six locations throughout the UK. It was mandatory for all managers to be at one of these meetings. The roadshow took about two hours. James Watson, Philip Mayo and I gave a slide and video presentation. It provided the background to the political discussions, explained the financial and banking arrangements, and gave indicative projections of what the shares might be worth if certain profit targets were met (although none of the projections forecast the level of actual success that was realized in the following five years). It explained the dealing arrangements and how they themselves could raise money to buy the shares. Finally, it asked them to fill in a form anonymously, so that we could judge whether we had a chance of success. The form simply asked three questions:

Are you in favour of the employee buy-out?

Will you 'sell' it down the line?

How much will you invest?

From the six meetings we knew that we had over 95 per cent support from this group. They *were* prepared to be agents by which we enthused the next 21,000 employees. They promised that they would on average invest more than £700 in the scheme.

With this level of support we knew we could aim for everyone in the business to receive at least three face-to-face presentations from their own management during the run-up to the buy-out. There is little doubt that much of the final decision-taking on whether to invest was as a result of word of mouth at the workplace – 'What do you think, governor?' 'I reckon it's worth a go.' 'If you feel that, so do I.'

We had a long communication schedule because we believed originally that the deal would be completed within six, not twelve, months. It was very difficult keeping interest and enthusiasm alive when we were running into legal troubles and we were missing deadlines.

We were fortunate to have Brian Cottee, a man of great ability, heading up our small internal communications department. He had spent most of his life in trade journalism and he came to us having been for a number of years the editor of our major industry journal, *Commercial Motor*. He was a marvellous simplifier – he could distil a complex concept into simple words that everyone could understand – and knew all about working to deadlines and working under pressure. He was not starry-eyed about the buy-out. He saw it as the best way forward and knew that he and his department would have to bear the major brunt of putting over the message.

We unashamedly wooed the media. We were more interested in getting coverage in the *Mirror*, the *Sun* and the *Daily Express* than in *The Times*, *Financial Times* and *Investors Chronicle*. The investors we wanted to influence were our drivers, clerks and pensioners who were more likely to read the popular tabloids than the heavies.

We therefore had to make the story one not only of business interest, but also of human interest. The tabloids do not waste much of their space on pure business coverage. We had to play to their interest in employee capitalism, driver-bosses, in the directors mortgaging their homes to buy the company. We stimulated debate – was it right for a man to have not only his job, his pension but also his savings all riding on the success of his company? The Union versus the Company view on investment and ownership was given a good airing. We also as directors recognized that our own personal finances and reasons for investment would be grist for the media mill. We never refused an interview, never refused to answer a question. We knew that the media coverage was vital to us. We were prepared to sup with the devil because he was integral to our success, but I hope we managed to use a long spoon.

Finally, the pension fund problem continued to haunt us. As we knew, the funds were significantly under-funded. Separate from the buy-out, the trustees of the funds, led by Victor Paige, the Deputy Chairman, were in deep negotiation with the ministry. Actuaries find it hard to agree. Their calculations of future pension obligations depend on the assumptions made. Assumptions cannot be proved – they can only reflect views on what might happen in the future to inflation and the real rate of return on equities. Other factors to take into account are the age profile and life expectancy of the workforce. The number of redundancies and early retirements which might be expected came into the equation. The government actuary and the NFC pension fund actuary bandied assumptions throughout the twelve months.

In the end it came to the usual horse trade with the ministry saying that they would not provide more than £48.7m to meet the pension deficiencies. The trustees were not satisfied, and reluctantly took the line that it was as a result of the buy-out that they were losing the full commitment of government to the pension schemes. They therefore looked to the new Consortium – as we would be called in the future – to meet in full the deficit. At a time when we were desperately short of adequate profits, we had to agree that for at least three years, and longer if necessary, we would contribute an extra £400,000 a year to the pension funds to help with the theoretical deficit. In the event the assumption (like most assumptions) turned out to be nothing like the reality. Inflation and the real yield on equities over the next eight years was much better than forecast. The pension fund today, like most funded schemes, has healthy surpluses. At the time we were not best pleased with the trustees. They had their job to do and they did it well, but it was nearly the straw that broke the camel's back. However, they did agree that if it was necessary for them to invest in NFC to ensure that the minimum of £4m equity was raised, they were prepared to buy up to 750,000 shares.

By November 1981 we had jumped all the barriers. At the last meeting before everything was finally put to bed, Barclays' negotiating team demanded an extra 2½ per cent of the equity because of all the extra work and cost involved in finding a way through. We were exhausted, and rather than argue any further we conceded the extra 2½ per cent – it didn't seem much at the time. Today that 2½ per cent is worth £23m!

At an emotional ceremony at our HQ in Bedford, in front of all the senior managers, Sir Peter Baldwin, the Permanent

Secretary, on behalf of the government, signed an option agreement to sell us the company for £53.5m, conditional upon our raising at least £4,125,000 (of which at least £2,125,000 had to be subscribed in cash other than through the Employee Loan Scheme) from the employees, families and pensioners.

Even this was not without its last-minute drama. Under a government reshuffle, Norman Fowler had moved on from Transport and David Howell had taken his place. We were then subjected to a month of indecision while the government decided whether it was prepared to sign the option, much of it being the natural delay which takes place when a new Secretary of State takes over. It would be Howell's decision, and he would have to justify his actions to parliament.

I was becoming angry at the delay. I decided with the agreement of the team to issue a final ultimatum. I thought we had all the cards. The government was publicly committed to the scheme, the banks were onside, the media were almost universally in favour. I went to see David Howell and socked it to him. The negotiated sale at £53.5m was our final offer, either he accepted it within seven days or the deal was off!

David Howell is a courteous and considerate man. He replied that he understood my anxiety to complete the deal but I had to understand that while he was in favour of the NFC buy-out, he had only that week received an alternative offer for the company at a higher price which he had to investigate further.

I felt like a man who had just had his royal flush called and beaten by four aces. I retired as gracefully as possible, expressing the hope that it would be possible for the Secretary of State to recognize that there was more at stake than mere money and that he would see his way graciously to sign the option agreement with us. Much later I found out that the alternative bid was from a consortium hastily cobbled together by General Motors involving a major US haulier. They saw the prospect of tying the supply of trucks to their ailing UK truck manufacturing operations. It was bound to fail as a haulier must be free to buy the tools of his trade from the best supplier.

Finally, the government gave us the go ahead. We had a clear run to the winning post – and the winning post was the establishment of the first major employee-owned business in the UK. The only comparable company was the partnership established in the 1930s by the forward-looking John Spedan Lewis. He decided that the John Lewis retail group should be passed in trust for the benefit of the employees. He believed that all employees should be treated as partners in the same way as lawyers and accountants. If the partnership prospered, the employees who had created the profits would share in them. Through an elaborate structure of elected committees, the employees were guaranteed a significant role in the decision-taking process of the partnership. However, while the profits belonged to the employees, John Spedan Lewis decided that the ownership of the business would rest in a trust. If the partnership could be valued today, it would be worth many hundreds of millions of pounds.

However, John Spedan Lewis did not invite the employees to take part in the capital ownership. This is the key difference. NFC would, if we could jump the last hurdle, be truly employee-owned, and the employees and their families would be genuinely free to do with their capital stakes as they wish.

All we now had to do was to raise a minimum of £4m. If this hurdle could not be jumped, then the bank finance would not be available. Barclays, who by this time had managed to syndicate the loans by involving four other banks, felt that without this minimum level of employee commitment, the concept they had been sold had no real validity. Below £4m, the employees would in effect have voted with their feet and, without their enthusiastic support, NFC on its historic track record was not a good investment. (It is ironic that the one financial institution that turned down the loan syndication should have been 3is – the company set up by other banks to encourage initiative. In fairness to them, they said it was not their kind of deal – too much medium-term loan and not enough equity sweeteners.)

We had been confident throughout that the employees would enthusiastically support the deal. But how could we really be sure? The major trade union was against it. More than one of the popular tabloids had advised against a person having his job and his capital at stake in the same business. Popular capitalism had not yet taken off – share ownership was not thought to be for the working class. When the prospectus was issued, many bankers and financial advisers advised their NFC clients not to invest. The offer was at least six months late, and the employees knew, earlier than the bankers, that all was not well with the company's trading.

It is hardly surprising that, with so much senior management time being taken up with the buy-out, profitability was declining. We had to revise our forecast three times in the last three months, always downwards. It was difficult to manage the business effectively as our objectives were in conflict. If we bought the company, we wanted to have sorted out as many of the problems as possible to give ourselves a flying start once we took over. This meant tackling more fiercely the problems of overmanning, and also repositioning some of the companies in their market places. Both required expensive courses of action – one in redundancy, the other in advertising and relocation costs. On the other hand, we had to present reasonable profits so that the banks could feel confident about lending and the government could be confident that the NFC would not go bankrupt within a few months of the buy-out. The senior managers felt trapped between the nutcrackers and a hard place.

It had been pointed out to us with all the solemnity that only corporate lawyers can summon that to forecast a profit out-turn in the prospectus and then to fail to make it was to risk an appearance at the Old Bailey. However, *not* to forecast meant that we had little to tempt in the marginal investor.

Profits were swinging around so much that we decided against producing a forecast. We believed we could persuade the NFC family to invest not just by offering financial gain, but also by showing them a vision of a better company. It did not make the banks any happier, though, and if anything it reduced their confidence.

I well remember us enjoying the company's Christmas dance. Company socials, usually held only once a year, are always fun. It is the one occasion when all the latent relationships which are suppressed by a formal business environment throughout the year can erupt to the surface. Whether a manager makes a fool of himself with a young secretary, or the office junior advises the board member where things are going wrong, it is always an enjoyable and lively affair. This particular year, a phone call for

107

James Watson, our Finance Director, from Michael Peterson of Barclays rudely interrupted the fun. The message was simple, straightforward and contained none of the festive spirit normally associated with the season of good will. 'One more reduction in the forecast out-turn and the deal is off.'

So we demanded of every company and every individual that profits be delivered as forecast, and the response was magnificent once it became clear to everyone that the buy-out depended on it.

Over Christmas and the New Year we kept on communicating. Yet more meetings at every workplace and with every shift. At last the prospectus emerged from its 49th edition and was passed by the lawyers as fit for investor consumption. It was full of wealth warnings such as 'shares can go down as well as up'. A final video was circulated. Leaflets explaining how to borrow money from banks and building societies were printed. The last touches were put to the terms on which the employees could borrow money. We introduced, fairly late in the day, a scheme whereby interest-free loans for £200 were made available to pay it back at £4 per week. The media were re-enthused, even though by this time they were showing signs that, because of the delays and the many false starts, the excitement had gone out of the story.

The offer for sale was open for three weeks. We could do nothing more than sit back and wait for the money to pour in. We sat back and waited . . . and waited . . . and waited. After twelve days, had a thermometer been put up outside the building – like a church when it is raising funds for a new roof – the mercury would not have risen above the bowl at the thermometer base. I began to think that I had presided over the biggest employee turn-down in business history. I even began surreptitiously to scan the job pages of the *Daily Telegraph*.

But in the last seven days, the money poured into the registrar's offices in Worthing. What our new owners had been doing should have been obvious. They were not going to raise the money for their investment until the deal was certain. Some then had to finalize the arrangements for loans with their bank managers after taking final advice from whomever they trusted. Some converted building society deposits into cheques to attach to the application form. Some sold shares to buy the new shares. Some had to persuade their parents, who couldn't invest, to lend them money to invest themselves. Some had to persuade family trusts that it was a sound proposition. Some were very canny – they did not want their cheques cashed until the last minute, thus saving one or two days' interest on the borrowings. It was hardly surprising that the money was late flowing in.

Having made up their minds, some trusted the post which at the time was suffering the aftermath of a go-slow. Others who did not, decided to deliver their applications personally to the registrar whose offices were located in a residential suburb of Worthing – a sleepy south coast holiday and retirement town. Traffic was disrupted as 30-ton lorries and 46-foot car trans-porters attempted to park while the drivers delivered their mates' application forms.

In the end the offer was well oversubscribed. When trying to assess what money to raise we decided the maximum we could reasonably expect the employees to raise was £6¼m. The bank's equity contribution raised the total amount of the issue to £7.5m. In the event the total subscribed by the NFC family was £7m. We therefore had the galling task, for a company that had loaded itself with debt, of returning money to the investors because of oversubscription. About 11,000 pensioners, employees, and their families had filled in the forms, raised the money, written the cheques and sent them in. NFC would at last belong to its employee family once two ceremonies were complete.

The formal legal ceremony came first. We assembled in a large room at the merchant bank, with one of the largest tables I had ever seen. When we walked in the table was fully covered and groaning under the weight of documentation. We then played the City version of bingo. Instead of numbers, a 'caller' – a solemn commercial lawyer – called out the names of legal documents. As each legal document was called, it was duly held up so that the board could acknowledge its presence. The document raised was duly noted in the formal minutes of the meeting and our attention moved on to what was going up next.

More than eighty documents were held in the air before the legal niceties had been completed, at which point a cheque for

£53.5m made out to the government was temporarily put in my hand. At this stage I thought I noted the doors being locked! It rested in my fingers for but a fleeting moment before I passed it to a senior civil servant who in turn handed me a rather unimpressive share certificate. The NFC was now legally ours. Champagne corks popped – but it was something of an anticlimax. A City office was not symbolic of NFC – we needed a ceremony in a transport depot.

In a great hurry over the weekend, we arranged for David Howell to carry out the public ceremony. We informed the media and they turned out in their droves. We invited representatives of all our companies. We lined up trucks from all our operations. When I met the drivers before the ceremony, I was surprised to see John McGleesham, one of the shop stewards from the Coventry depot of Cartransport. He had a reputation for being bloody-minded and difficult in the past. I said, 'What on earth are you doing here, John?' He replied, 'I'm enthusiastic about the concept, and I've invested. It should be a great new beginning for NFC.' It was the first taste of many attitude changes that were to come in the future.

We chose the Fashionflow depot in Camden for the ceremony. It was a fitting location. It had been an old railway goods yard. NFC had modernized the premises to provide an upmarket distribution centre for Marks & Spencer – the customer who more than any other had taught us that quality of service was where our future lay.

The ceremony was simple but very emotional for many of us there. The key players in the buy-out spoke in turn: Tom Camoys of Barclays Merchant Bank who first recognized the excitement of the vision and found the cash to support it. Bobbie Lawrence, our Chairman, who had backed us throughout and had handled the many political problems. I spoke for the team. My first observation was that, in traditional banking style, the cheque had been made out for £53.5m – only! I went on to outline a future where we would get rid of the 'us and them' attitude between management and employees and substitute for it an 'us and us'. Employees as owners would be working together to create and share wealth. Finally, David Howell, who together with Norman Fowler had had the political will to make it happen, said, 'There is nothing so powerful as an idea whose time has come.'

The concept of employee ownership and control of a major national company was in being. The theory was over, it was now our jobs to make it work . . .

In many ways the twelve months I have described were the most exciting and challenging of my business life. At the same time they were the saddest. The day we announced our intention to buy the company, my wife Pat went to her doctor and breast cancer was diagnosed. During the whole of the year she supported me totally, knowing she was losing her own personal battle. She died in March 1983. Fate was cruel. I have found it hard even to this day to come to terms with her death. Why, after all the support she gave to me and the family, was she not allowed to live to enjoy the rewards of the buy-out and to see the success that her children have made of their lives? It is the question the bereaved always asks, and to which there is no adequate answer.

6

Making it Work –
Employees as Shareholders

'. . . we are always looking out for the extra
shining penny – the harder we work, the
more we earn.'

NFC employee, BBC Radio 4,
'The World at One', 22 February 1982

'Where there is no vision the people perish.'
Proverb

I woke up on 10 February 1982 to the realization that we were
on the first day of a very long haul. We were not short of
messages of good will. I received this telex from one of our depots
in Essex:

We've shot the shop steward, topped up the tanks,
checked the tyres, oil and water and cleaned the win-
dows. So keep to the nearside and keep your elbows in,
we're going out to earn some divi!

Our reply was:

We have put away the champagne, sent fraternal greet-
ings to the TGWU, arranged for interest rates to drop,
and are well on the way to the first interim dividend.

(Perhaps it was a sign that the gods of business were with us
when the interest rates dropped ½ per cent the first day of our
ownership of the company.)

We had coined a new slogan to help us on our way, 'We
are in the driving seat', and we plastered it over every vehicle

and depot. The excitement was real and infectious. Attitudes would change, and were already changing. A truck driver visiting one of our depots in Oldham saw a parcel standing in the open getting wet. He shouted at the handling staff to get it out of the rain, finishing his outburst with the words, 'Of course I care, I'm a shareholder.' The press picked up many stories of staff turning off lights and beginning to give a little extra customer service. We had to seize this good will, channel it and make a success of running a company owned by its workforce.

We had few precedents to follow – The Wedgwood-Benn cooperatives set up in the 1970s (Meredon, Scottish Daily News and Kirkby Manufacturing Equipment) had not been a conspicuous success. They had been based on the concepts of equality and consensus. Decisions were only taken if everyone agreed, and there was no hierarchical management structure. This would not be our route ahead, we had to have strong management and a sharp decision-taking process.

I had read about a successful cooperative venture, in the Basque region of Spain, called Mondragon – a group of industrial cooperatives which had expanded into finance, agriculture and education. It was very different from NFC, but what seemed to have made it successful was that it recruited, or found within its ranks, good managers. These managers were elected annually by the shareholders (who were the workers) to manage the business on a day-to-day basis. At the end of each year the managers reported to the worker shareholders on their stewardship. At this meeting the managers raised any major issues of policy and then invited the shareholders to elect them to manage for a further year.

On reflection, never mind about a cooperative, this is what any public company should be about. At the annual general meetings, the directors give an account of their activities during the year to the shareholders; they then invite the shareholders to elect them to be directors for another year. The normal company AGM therefore had the legal framework to be the centrepiece for our kind of employee ownership. Yet AGMs in the main have not been successful in securing shareholder involvement. This is primarily as a result of the average shareholder's indifference to the way a company is managed. Many boards have not welcomed shareholder involvement, and many company chairmen take pride in their ability to complete an AGM in the least possible time. The record probably stands at well under three minutes. Only when things are going wrong do the shareholders turn up in force to question the board. But this makes the average shareholder the equivalent of an absentee landlord. He owns a piece of the company and, so long as he is getting his annual 'rent' in the form of dividends and capital growth, he really does not need to visit the 'farm'. This is even more the case when the 'owner' of the shares is not an individual but a financial institution which 'owns' the shares on behalf of its clients, whether pensioners or insured persons.

One way ahead for us was to make our AGM work in the way originally intended by the legislators who framed company law. Our worker shareholders were far from absentee landlords. If we returned to basics and made our AGMs meaningful, our employees would be actively involved not only in the election of their leaders but also in the major policy decisions vital to the future development of their company.

Before we considered how we should treat shareholders, we had to decide how we would manage the business in the new situation. First, we had to decide how we should treat our employees. We were clear that share ownership could not 'buy' an individual employment privileges. We had to keep share ownership and employment separate. While we believed that employment attitudes would change with share ownership, we could not make ownership of shares a condition of employment. So, if an individual was to be appraised for promotion, the amount of shares he held could not be a consideration. Promotion had to be on merit. Similarly, if redundancy was declared, share ownership had no part to play in the decision of who had to leave the company. The directors understood this well, but the employee shareholders were less willing to accept it. I receive many letters about employment issues. They start, 'As a share-holder, I think you should know . . .' Mostly the issue has nothing to do with shareholding. I usually have to reply that we have well-established personnel policies to sort out employment grievances. (Nevertheless, it does give me, as Chairman, an insight as to how our personnel and management policies are being implemented!)

How was our treatment of employees to be different in the future? One thing was certain, we had to use the skills that we had acquired as communicators during the buy-out to make sure that our employees were the best-informed workforce in the UK. Communication, however, should not be dictated solely from the centre. We required company managements to communicate directly with their employees, and not – as in the past – mainly through the trade union negotiation and consultative machinery. We set an example from the top by making sure that we had an open communicative management style. The Head of Communications was required to attend all executive board meetings – he then knew of all the key issues that were being discussed. Each month he prepared a broadsheet of items which should be communicated down the line. The companies then added any items of interest from their management meetings and passed the information down to the branch manager. This, together with branch information, was the basis for briefings held at least monthly at the depots. We were, I realize, following the system used and hallowed through decades by the church. Parish magazines normally contain a general, spiritual message from the archbishop, a diocesan message from the bishop and, most of all, news of what is happening in the parish from the vicar. Ours was a similar system, although nobody is claiming equal spiritual wisdom with the Archbishop of Canterbury.

Six times a year the Head of Communications prepared and circulated to all depots the 'NFC Manager', which covered all the key events of the business. To this communication system we added the participative management style and reward system which was already in position and which I have already described. We had also introduced in the late 1970s an overlapping triangle system to improve communication. This simply meant that the boss of each layer of management served on the board or committee that managed the group or division of which his business was a part. So the company managing director served on the group board. The group MD served on the NFC executive board and the chief executive served on the main board. Each agenda at all levels had a standing item covering what had happened on the superior board.

Any policy issue was always passed down the line for discussion before a decision was taken on high. In that way any nonsenses were revealed and a large number of management had taken part in the debate before any major decision was taken. It was slow, but it then made implementation of the policies that much easier.

Together, properly used, these systems should ensure that we have a wholly involved and well-informed workforce. It would be idle to pretend the system is perfect. Some companies and individuals are naturally good communicators. Some are still authoritarian and believe knowledge is power – so why share it? Involvement and communication is a garden that needs constant attention – allow it to be neglected and the weeds will quickly grow.

Our next concern was the trade unions. Where would they fit into the new culture? We hoped that they would want to share our vision of the future. If they did, their role would be different but we thought the new role might form a blueprint for trade unionism in the twenty-first century. It needed them to make the same change in attitude that we had made. It required them to put at the top of their agenda the creation of wealth. The union negotiating role would then be focused on the sharing of the wealth that was created.

It is a great sadness that this attitudinal change has not taken place. The unions still see their prime and almost sole role as that of negotiating wages and conditions. They are uncertain and suspicious of the world of employee capitalism. They have proved reluctant to move away from their role as guardians of fair play for all, and unwilling to move into the world of reward for achievement – putting the individual centre stage, evaluating *him*, and concentrating upon *his* needs and development. Trade unionism has traditionally concentrated on the group, using the collective strength of the group to obtain a better deal from management.

Trade unions are cautious of change and have rarely wanted to be part of the process of evolving change. Sharing the wealth that is created through share ownership and profit-sharing is not of their world. They prefer to concentrate upon basic pay – money up front, not money once wealth has been created. Profit-sharing in shares is less acceptable than profit-sharing in money – unless the votes of those shares can be exercised by the union. An employee voice on the board is acceptable if the individual is a nominee of the union. All these attitudes would have had to have changed if the trade unions were to march in step with employee ownership.

Regrettably we have not marched very far together, and our relationships with our unions remain much as they always were. The only major change has been that wage bargaining has been decentralized to the operating companies, which is where it should be. The wage deal is now struck at the level where productivity bargaining has some relevance. The company managements know both what they want and what they can afford, which was never the case when NFC settled its wage deals in the centre.

We still have closed-shop agreements. We have never sought to alter these as they do not really stand in the way of our employing the quality of people we need. But even with the protection of closed-shop agreements, union membership in NFC among all grades is on the decline. In the clerical and management grades where no closed shop exists, union membership has declined to the point where it is nonsense for the union to say that they represent the employees in most of our companies. For example, membership in Pickfords Travel had dropped to about 4 per cent when we decided to withdraw union negotiating rights. With a membership of only 4 per cent, the union clearly could not claim that they spoke for the majority of the employees.

At NFC level we tried for the first four years to involve the trade unions in a dialogue about the future strategy of the business. We have now given up the initiative. The general secretaries of some of the unions could not give the meetings the necessary priority in their diaries. Where should the priorities of general secretaries lie? In the UK trade unions see themselves as having an important political role to play. Priority is given to dealing with the Labour Party, the International Labour Union, and their own TUC. This leaves key union leaders little time to deal with the future of the companies in which their members work. Their busy political schedules meant that only occasionally could they all turn up for NFC strategy meetings. Surely trade union priorities should be to ensure that their members work for well-managed and forward-thinking companies that are capable of competing on a world scale? Few trade union leaders today seem to regard this as their top priority. Much more important for them is to ensure that the UK has the right political environment in which trade unions can flourish. Trade unionism in the 1990s must surely concentrate on the process of wealth creation and much less on the political environment in which it is created.

Even when the general secretaries were able to attend, there was no meeting of minds over strategy. The strategy by which we would develop our distribution activities was to gain marketing edge by improving the productivity of the operations we had, or were planning to take over – mainly from companies who did their own distribution. This strategy did not appeal to our union friends. In the immortal words of the Hull-born TGWU Commercial Trades Officer, 'We are agin it!' They preferred their members to be highly paid for poor productivity with existing employers. In this way more short-term employment was created. They would not face up to the question of whether the long-term interests of their members would be better served by working for efficient, world-class companies. Remaining the guardians of inefficient practices cannot be the right stance for trade unions in the 1990s.

My personal disillusionment with trade unionism was compounded by their response to our need to merge two loss-making businesses, the Parcels operations of Roadline and National Carriers. Roadline was organized by the TGWU, National Carriers by the NUR. We presented three options to the unions for discussion: close National Carriers with the loss of 2500 jobs; close Roadline with the loss of a similar number of jobs; or merge the two with the loss of 1000 jobs. Jimmy Knapp of the NUR immediately chose the option which resulted in the least job losses. Reasonably, he sought equal representation with the TGWU in the merged company. Ron Todd of the TGWU was of similar mind. However, the TGWU is a devolved union.

There was no will further down the union hierarchy to carry out the General Secretary's wishes. The TGWU officials involved in the negotiations made it clear that they were not interested in merger – they opted to close National Carriers. They were not even prepared to sit down in the same room as the NUR negotiators to talk about a merger. They were hell bent not on job preservation but on the maintenance of their control over the negotiations and membership rights in our Parcels business.

Faced with this impasse, management unilaterally took the decision. We decided to close Roadline, preserving as much business as was viable and transferring as many Roadline employees into the new company as possible. Negotiating rights were given to the NUR.

Despite the weakening of trade union influence, the average earnings of our employees have advanced in real terms each year. We are progressing towards being a single-status company. We have introduced a new single-status pension scheme so that everyone is treated equally on retirement. Previously, we had a good scheme for the salaried employees and an ungenerous scheme for the hourly paid. But even the concept of single status which we now have is at odds with the union view of single status. To them, single status means everyone being paid a salary and everyone having similar pension arrangements – nothing else much changes. To us, single status is about everyone behaving and being rewarded in the same way as our managers. It means working, within reason, for whatever time and in whatever pattern is necessary to give service to our customers. Superior service is the only thing that will give us competitive edge. But, on the other hand, it means that the individual has rights: the right to create his own objectives, the right to being appraised, the right to receiving a remuneration package which reflects his personal contribution to the business, the right to training to update his skills, the right to a decent pension, the right to share in the capital growth of the company, the right to involvement in decisions that affect his work. It is hardly surprising that negotiations about single status in BRS did not get anywhere. Mind you, it was not merely a problem of union perceptions. Among our own management there were some who did not wish to take on the more difficult management style that my definition of single status entails.

The unions, therefore, have failed to grasp the new role that they could have played in the development of NFC since the buy-out. The cultural sea-change has sadly been too great for them to make. I hope in the future that a belief in wealth creation and a focus on the needs of the individual will become more important in trade union philosophy, than fairness, conflict, and the primacy of group strength.

The new board was not starry eyed. We believed that by becoming more employee-focused, communicating better, and involving employees in share ownership and policy-making it would take us some of the way, but equally we knew that that was not enough in itself to ensure success. We had to have clear vision and good strategies. Shortly after the takeover I reminded the board that we had to have a look at the longer-term direction of the business.

In the meantime we had a short-term problem that had to be addressed. How could we reduce debt? It is the natural reaction of prudent men, when faced with the mountain of debt that we had taken on, to want to reduce it. Most leveraged buy-outs (as they are now known in the US) look around to see which parts of the company they can sell to help in the debt-reduction programme. It is all part of a never-ending cycle of business life. Companies start small, are efficient, and expand. As a result of their success, they get a larger share of the market they understand well. They are rewarded with a high stock market rating – their shares are highly valued. With a high value on their equity and pressure for ever-increasing earnings per share, they decide to diversify and go down the well-worn trail of acquisition. In a relatively short time the company becomes a conglomerate. They are less successful managing in markets they neither know well nor understand. Their share price falls. They then fall prey to a takeover or a leveraged buy-out. The predator may be their own management, or it may be a company or group of businessmen who buy the company mainly through borrowings in the belief that the parts when sold are worth more than the market value of the whole. The predator needs to reduce his debt so he sells the peripheral activities and the company returns to its core activities. It does well, and it decides to diversify . . . The cycle can be pedalled endlessly round this business track. But the process of reducing debt by selling off parts of the business was not open to us. How could we invite employees to invest their savings and to join the family of shareholders, and then callously sell some of them out of the family? Employee-owned companies have to forgo some of the business weapons that are available to the normal company. In their place, however, we have employee commitment – worth more, we believe, than a quiverful of conventional business arrows.

In order to get the debt down, we turned for the first year to rationalizing properties. In every major town we usually had five properties: Pickfords Removals, BRS, National Carriers and Roadline would all have a presence, and Tankfreight, Cartransport, Waste Management and Tempco in selected cities would swell the number of locations.

We made each executive board member responsible for rationalizing a major city. We set up working groups to see how we might make better use of property by operating more than one company out of a single location. In the environment of state ownership the process would have been like drawing teeth. Pickfords and BRS operating together was just not on! Different cultures don't mix – neither do different unions. BRS and National Carriers just can't cohabit. But taboos break down when management from different companies have the common purpose of making the parent NFC successful. The difference was that their money was now invested in the parent. Property rationalization proceeded apace. We had to pay our dividend and meet our interest charges primarily from property sales in the first year. The companies even found that they enjoyed working with each other.

If attitudes are to change the first attitude change has to be seen from management. The need to survive in 1982/83 certainly saw a major change in NFC management attitudes. Management at all levels were taking the first step down the path of being as concerned for and as proud of the achievements of the whole as they were of their individual companies. My thoughts went back over twelve months to the meeting with the Pickfords

121

management in Bedford. Attitudes were on the march! But the short term had to lead to the long term. NFC had to have a clear long-term vision that had been carefully worked out.

A company's long-term vision can only come from the leader. That is not to say that he does not need much additional input, nor that it cannot be a shared vision – indeed, if the vision is totally shared the leader has done his job. He has succeeded in getting everyone to whistle the same tune. But it is most import-ant for *him* to recognize the need for a vision, and to be in the forefront of formulating and promoting it. Strategy emerges from the vision – strategy is merely the way in which the vision is realized. It is no good believing that any of this can be subcon-tracted to the corporate planning department. They can help. They can organize the planning system. They can do the research to validate the strategy. But the formulation of the vision, and keeping it bright and shining, rests with the leader. It is his most important job. Some do this instinctively, and do not perhaps make such a meal of it as I do. Others work at it, recognizing its absolute importance. Regrettably, many leaders of businesses do not even recognize the need for a vision of the future. Success to them is about doing deals – buying and selling companies, manipulating the bottom line. The lack of vision and hence leadership is all too obvious in their businesses.

We had to work out a long-term strategy. I put together an interesting group with cross-hierarchical and cross-functional backgrounds. We had two non-executive directors, two younger line managers, two executive main board members and the head of corporate planning. We first met in the autumn of 1982 with the target of giving birth to the new strategy by the summer of 1983.

At the first meeting I asked, 'Which of you have ever prepared a long-term strategy before?' The silence was deafening and I realized we were all novices at the game. Of course, we had prepared three-year plans – but a strategy to last a decade was outside our experience. We decided we should go to school to learn how other companies set about it. We wrote to a dozen business leaders who had built successful companies in their own lifetime. All responded positively and agreed to see us. To make sure we had the full range of experience open to us, we also wrote to the chairmen of two companies that, in our judgement, had lost their strategic way. You can often learn more by studying failure than by analysing success. Of course, we did not reveal our reasons for wanting to see those two chairmen, but it perhaps says something that neither of them agreed to see us!

Among others we had long discussions with Lord Sieff of Marks & Spencer, Sir Ernest Harrison of Racal, Sir Maxwell Joseph of Grand Metropolitan, Sir Owen Green of BTR and Gerald Ronson of Heron. All had different management styles, were operating in different markets and had different values. All had built successful and respected businesses. We were looking for the common denominator. We concluded it was that they had a clearer view of where they wanted their companies to go. They were also more determined to get there. Some of them would not embrace the word, but I concluded that they all had a very clear vision for their businesses, and that they mostly had clearly articulated business values.

At the same time, we worshipped at the feet of the corporate strategy gurus. We attended seminars being addressed by Michael Porter, Igor Ansoff, Michael Kami, et al. We sought the advice of business schools and consultancy practices specializing in strategy. We were usually depressed after these sessions with the academics and the advisers. The process of arriving at a long-term strategy in their view started from analysis: analysis of market position, of strengths and weaknesses; analysis of competitive and financial strength; analysis of customers and customer dependence. Out of this analysis would emerge the way forward. They were probably right intellectually, but the old tag of 'analysis to paralysis' more than once crossed our minds.

We decided to leave the theorists and to follow in the wake of the business winners. We went into the vision business. Each member of the working group agreed to write down his vision of NFC. It was to be in the form of a 'mission' statement. In this way everyone's vision would not only have to describe the business Paradise towards which we should be working, but would also have to indicate the path that we might take to get there. There was a surprising unanimity in these mission statements, and it was therefore not too difficult to get the group to accept mine! – albeit with some significant amendments.

We had to gather other important inputs. We were trying to create a company which would be acceptable to our new owners – the employees and pensioners. They therefore had to have an input. So we commissioned a survey (the first of many in future years) from MORI – Bob Worcester's market research company. We felt that he had, through his political opinion polls, advanced the difficult art of determining attitudes towards concepts.

We wanted the employees to tell us what kind of company *they* wanted. When I announced at the first AGM that we would carry out this survey by using a sample of 1000 shareholders, the reaction from the floor was that this was too important an issue to be trusted to a sample – why could not everyone have the opportunity of contributing to the debate? To poll everyone was more expensive and Bob Worcester advised us that it would not necessarily be more statistically significant than having a well-structured sample of 1000. But if our shareholders wanted to have a say, it would have been wrong for us to prevent them. If they were to be convinced that NFC was their company, they had to know that their views were listened to before policy was formulated.

It is of course difficult to solicit views on as complex an issue as corporate strategy. All we could do was to paint six or seven possible strategic scenarios and describe the type of company that would emerge from the strategy selected. We then asked the shareholders to indicate their preference. It mattered little that their preferred choice turned out not to be the preferred strategy that the working party recommended. It meant that we had to be able to explain with more conviction why our strategy was superior. Involvement does not mean the acceptance of the most popular view, for that would deny leadership.

Having started with a vision of where we would like to be, we then told the subsidiary companies how we saw them fitting into this picture. They were told whether they were development companies whom we were prepared to support not only in their organic growth but also, if necessary, by acquiring companies to make them more dominant in their market. The majority of companies were to be core businesses which we expected to

124

grow by their own efforts, and at the same time to provide cash to enable the development companies to acquire. There were also some sick businesses whose role was to heal themselves by reducing to a size where profitability was possible. Each company was then invited to spend a day with us and either to confirm or argue against our assessment. If they argued against, we asked them to concentrate their arguments mainly on showing that we had not fully understood the dynamics of the future growth of their market. We argued that, given a ten-year time horizon, if the market was good and we understood it, we should be able to allocate the resources (particularly good management – that scarcest resource of all) so that we would become a significant and profitable player. The discussions with the companies were intense – they knew the stakes were high.

We did not forget the employee shareholders. We spent much time thinking about and developing plans for motivating employees. Our new ownership concentrated our minds on this aspect of strategy. Before the buy-out it should have been more obvious than it was that in a service industry, without too much high technology, people were the means of gaining a marketing edge. High service levels were imperative and these would only be achieved by a first-class management working with employees who would accept, welcome and even promote change.

When we had harvested everyone's input, we then revisited our mission statement to see whether we really had the means of delivering the mission. We marginally changed the original vision in the light of this review of our capabilities. We next took the partially-completed strategy on a consultation tour. It involved, of course, the main board, the executive board and the top one hundred managers. Less obviously, we then took the strategy to a series of meetings around the country to which we invited all shareholders so that they could take part in the debate. Amendments were made as a result of this process. Finally, in early 1984, it was endorsed by the board.

It was a long slow process, I agree. But at the end of it *anyone* who wished to contribute had had a chance to do so. Everyone who wished to know knew what was in it. If it achieved nothing else, we believed the process would, and in fact did, make the implementation of the strategy that much easier. We were able to justify every future action we took by referring to the strategy which the shareholders had endorsed.

For example, part of our strategy was to develop our overseas activities which were negligible in 1982 into being 25 per cent of our earnings by 1990. This meant acquisitions. The money and management for the acquisitions had to come from the UK companies. New depots and new trucks in the UK had to be delayed while we improved the strength of the business by overseas investment which reduced our dependence on the UK economy. Before the strategy and the reasons for it had been explained, we had had questions about this move at the AGM and at shareholder meetings. Once the strategy was agreed, the questions stopped.

How much the buy-out and the consideration of long-term strategy changed top management can be seen when you consider the mission statement we made to support the 1981 plan which was addressed to our then owners, the government.

> The NFC is mainly a UK freight business. It will become more diversified into activities which in the main develop out of existing freight operations. It will also be internationalized. It will do this by establishing free-standing businesses. The aim is to secure sustained growth in earnings and net worth per share for its shareholders.

Fine as far as it went, but it lacked any real vision. It did not recognize that the best competitive weapon we had was our employees. The focus changed as our ownership changed. This is the 1988 mission statement:

> NFC will seek to become a company for all seasons. It will achieve this by developing a broad-based, international transport, distribution, travel and property group with a high reputation for service in all its activities. It will retain its commitment to widespread employee control. It will have a participative style associated with first-class results-orientated employment packages. It will seek increased employment opportunities and real growth of dividends and share values for its shareholders.

126

It has vision, but above all over half the statement concentrates on how we will become a high-service business by motivating our employees and satisfying our worker shareholders. We also commit ourselves to maintaining the unique employee owner-ship and control which in turn gives us marketing edge. This part of the mission statement was to cause some problems to the City when we sought a quotation on the London Stock Exchange in 1989.

The product strategies that emerged were arrived at before Tom Peters and Robert Waterman's book *In Search of Excellence* identified the essentials that make companies excellent. 'Sticking to the knitting', high service levels, people-focused, pride of product were already part of our vision. We decided we would stick with the services we knew – and we were lucky that they were all growth markets. We would make the companies, whose market sectors were clearly defined, responsible for following the market trends and adapting their services to where their market noses took them. There was to be no leaping of fences into services we did not understand, but equally no creation of artificial fences to prevent our managers developing new services that they felt the customers would buy. We had learnt our lesson from the restrictions to which we were subjected when we were state-owned.

Follow your customers – or, better still, anticipate their needs and be in front of their demands – was the goal. To do this they would need to control their own marketing, employee remuneration and motivation packages, engineering and capital spending (within agreed annual limits, of course). So this enabled us to redefine the role of the centre. We could never be a pure holding company, but we realized our role in the future had to be strategic. We would tell the companies what game and on which pitch they were playing; that is, we would define and limit the market they were in. We would be the referee. As all the companies were broadly involved in the transport and logistics business, there were bound to be overlaps. In fact, in distribution, the biggest market of all in which we were small players, we needed to be bigger and therefore had three companies compet-ing in this market.

Having been brought up in Unilever where they frequently

had more than one brand playing in a single market of detergents or frozen foods, I found no problem with this untidiness. Unilever argued, and I agree, that by having two brands, it gives you a potentially larger market share. It was often the case that a customer putting his distribution out for third-party tender would in the end be choosing between the different solutions offered by two NFC companies.

We told the companies what resources they could have. The macho contest was usually about capital – the argument should really have focused on which of the top one hundred managers we were prepared to allocate. Control over allocation of this precious resource rests with the centre.

Apart from this, the centre monitored performance – usually on a quarterly basis assuming the company was broadly on target. We approved the corporate plans, their strategies and the budgets.

From the strategic study emerged the products, the people policies and the organizational structure, so we were all set, we hoped, for success. However, we had to match good business strategies with an imaginative programme for ensuring share-holder involvement.

The eleven thousand shareholders with which we started could be divided into three different groups. Firstly, there were the banks. They owned 17½ per cent of the equity and we were required to report to them quarterly. Their major concern was that we should not break any of the 21 covenants we had agreed to as a condition of the loan. The covenants were all-embracing and were usually commercial business ratios. The most signifi-cant of these was interest cover – the number of times that the interest we were committed to pay them was covered by the profits before interest. This covenant became tougher with time. It started in the first full year at 1.5 times and progressed to 2. The other covenant which was particularly important to them was the gearing covenant. Here the banks wanted to place a limit on the total borrowings which the group could undertake from the banks themselves and elsewhere to cover the money that they had lent us. The covenant was a gearing level on balance sheet of not more than 1¼ times. That meant our total borrowings were not to be more than 1¼ times what we owned after we had deducted all the money we owed. Our communication with the bankers was regular and numerate. Each quarter we invited them to a meeting at which the progress of the company was reported, and our performance against the covenants was demonstrated.

My impression was that over the years the bankers had become so expert at closing every conceivable loophole by which a borrower could undermine the asset base on which they had lent, that some of the covenants had become so complex not even all the bankers understood them. There was one covenant which I confess I never understood and which we never managed to meet. After about eighteen months the bankers and our finance director finally agreed that the covenant was impossible! It goes to show that when you are as desperate as we were to do the deal, the fine print sometimes gets neglected.

We always invited this group of shareholders to our annual meetings and gave them special treatment. They, I believe, enjoyed them as much as any of the other shareholders. Over the years when we wanted to give advantages to our employee shareholders at the expense of non-employees – which of course included the banks – we never found them unwilling to go along with the idea provided they saw it would add to employee commitment.

The other 82½ per cent of the equity was held by employees, families and the pensioners. In the early years we used the same methods to involve this group. We had decided early on that we should, if possible, pay dividends quarterly. This meant that the financial results had to be reported to the shareholders quarterly. We used these emerging quarterly results as the major substance of a shareholder letter. This, through time, grew in size and substance to cover all items of interest in the business. Quarterly results and dividends also allowed the external valuer to decide the 'fair' price at which the shares could change hands at the dealing days. Philip Mayo recognized that we had to have some means by which shareholders who wanted to buy or sell shares could trade with each other. If there had not been a disciplined system to supervise the share trading, individual trading would have broken out and the control over it would have been impossible. So we wrote into the articles of association the rules by which our internal stock market would work. All transactions would be through a share trust – the members of which would be elected by the shareholders on a one-man one-vote basis. We did not want the big shareholders dominating the trust.

The external valuer's methods of valuation were never formally declared, but through time the valuations became more weighted towards the estimated value of the shares had the company been listed on the Stock Exchange – less a discount because we were not so listed. The stock market price of any share is determined not only by its historic performance but more particularly on its expected future performance. Recognizing this, the board took the decision always to communicate to shareholders their 'best view' of the next twelve months' trading so the 'family' investors could decide whether to buy or sell with as much knowledge of future trading prospects as the board. 'Insider' trading by senior management could not be allowed to happen in our type of company. We did not want someone at the AGM saying, 'I noticed, Chairman, you bought shares. Was this because you knew something that I as a junior employee did not?' Whether or not to continue with the 'best view' after we were listed on the Stock Exchange was the cause of great argument later in the saga, because the conventional wisdom is that quoted companies must at all cost avoid making a forecast.

With knowledge of the current results, the dividends, the valuer's price and the best view of the future, our shareholders were in a position to decide each dealing day whether to buy or sell. The share trust then matched buyers and sellers according to a set of priorities that had been thrashed out by the shareholders in the meetings in the first year.

If we were to engender trust from the shareholders when it came to share dealings, the board had to be like Caesar's wife, above suspicion. The first test of this came when the employees subscribed for far more shares than were available at the buy-out. How should we allocate the available shares and who should be cut back? The board unanimously agreed that any subscription for shares to the value of over £50,000 should be cut back to £50,000. After this everyone subscribing for over 600 shares should be cut back by 7 per cent.

The board members felt that this was unfair to them as individuals. The directors had taken the personal financial risk of the buy-out; if as a result of the prospectus anyone claimed that they had been misled or that it was incorrect, the legal liability lay personally with the directors. The banks had insisted that the directors invested at least £25,000 each, otherwise the deal was off. In these circumstances it seemed unfair that the directors should be cut back in the same way as all the other investors who had not had to take any risks.

I agreed with this view at first, and sought counsel from Ron Watson of Barclays. His advice was pure gold. He argued that the directors must from the start lead by example – they must not seek privilege. His view was that we should have our investment cut back in exactly the same way as anyone else. He was right and on reflection we agreed without much argument. I did mention to him recently that at the current price of shares his piece of 'advice' had now cost me £1.2m. He didn't weep or even offer to buy me a beer! Do what's right and shame the devil!

At the first AGM the shareholders were vociferous on the subject of who had priority to buy shares on dealing days. Throughout the seven years that the internal dealing system lasted, there were always – with one exception – more buyers than sellers. Incidentally, the one exception was not the dealing day after Black Monday in 1987. NFC's price did not escape the general savaging all shares received, and was valued at the following dealing day 14 per cent lower. It was the first time the price had ever fallen. The reaction of our shareholders was that the City had got it wrong – NFC was a good company and there was no underlying sense to the reduction. On that dealing day we had one of the highest percentage of buyers to sellers that we were ever to experience.

The arguments put forward about who should have priority over available shares went two ways. As Ken Lucas, one of our most supportive but more outspoken shareholders, put it, 'We supported you at the beginning when others didn't. Now because we already have shares we are at the bottom of the pile when it comes to getting more.' Ken was a supervisor at our Hull parcels depot. He was not a man to mince words. Unfortunately, some two years later his branch was closed and he was made redundant due to the rationalizing of the parcels operations. But each year he turns up at the AGM and always makes valid comments about the board's performance. Even if his Yorkshire comments at times cause us embarrassment. For example, in 1988 when we had taken an option to buy a US company and then decided not to go ahead at a cost of £5m, he asked, 'Are there no whiz kids on the board who could have spotted that the company was no good? If we had spent £5m on the parcels company three years ago I might still have a job with NFC!'

My argument on share allocation was that we had to persuade the 13,000 employees who did not invest in the beginning to join the family. So if they did apply they must be welcomed like prodigal sons and be given priority to buy any shares that were available. If we acquired a company, those new employees must similarly be given the opportunity of joining the family as quickly as possible.

The compromise finally agreed was that the needs of first-time buyers would be met in part by issuing new shares. Existing shareholders could buy more shares after the first-time buyers' needs were met. The needs of the smaller buyers who already held shares would, other things being equal, be met in full. The big players would be savagely cut back. The outcome at the end of each dealing day was usually that all requests for up to 1000 or 1200 shares were met. In this way it became very difficult for any individual to acquire a significant percentage of the company. The largest personal shareholder owns less than ½ per cent of NFC. But this, we argued, is what wider share ownership should be all about – preventing a concentration of shares ending up in too few hands. There was always, from the beginning, an active internal market in the shares and at its peak some £18m of shares changed hands in one year. Every dealing day when the new trading price was announced, it provided a new wave of interest.

Keeping the shareholders involved and interested was our on-going objective. To this end we decided that the shareholders must have a regular forum at which they could talk to board members. Each board member was therefore like a Member of Parliament, allocated a constituency. The country was divided into ten and each of us was given the task of visiting our own particular constituency at least four times a year – it frequently was more often than this if there were key policies to discuss. Major towns in each area were selected and shareholders were invited to attend. The meetings were always after normal working hours on weekday evenings. The attendance varied but normally around eighty people would attend each meeting.

The board member would give a presentation of the results to the shareholders, and raise any other current issues. He would then invite questions, comments or criticisms. Minutes were kept of all meetings and they were circulated to all executive board members. In this way we were receiving feedback on any issues worrying the shareholders. As always, these were mixed, and were certainly not confined to 'shareholder' matters. In the early days at my meetings I did try to confine the issues to those which really were shareholder matters, but of course everyone was there not only as a shareholder but also as an employee or a pensioner. It was impossible to rule out personnel, operational and marketing matters.

At one of my first regional meetings in London, one of our truck drivers, a small, perky Cockney, stood up and said, 'Governor, why is it that my opposite number from Newcastle, who I am supposed to change over with at Doncaster, is never on time?' (The way many of the overnight services were organized was on a changeover basis: the driver from London brought the truck as far as Doncaster, where he met up with the southbound driver from Newcastle. They changed trucks and then went back to their respective home bases. In this way expensive overnight payments were avoided and the drivers always slept in their own beds!)

'Fred,' I asked, 'is that really a shareholder's question?'

'Well, gov, I am a shareholder and it certainly is a question.'

Absolutely irrefutable logic! But we had to be careful never to make either operational or personnel decisions, otherwise we would clearly have been undermining the authority of local management. Nevertheless, if a business or employment issue was raised, we tried to make certain that the answer was passed back via the local management as quickly as possible.

It is argued that the level of interest in the regional meetings is not sufficient to justify the directors' time. In an average year, probably as few as four thousand shareholders, out of between thirty and forty thousand on today's register, actually attend. I disagree. I believe it gives everyone the opportunity of raising issues, and if they do not attend it means that they are satisfied with the information they are getting and with the way the company is being run. If they do attend, it may be they are only there to meet up with old friends. But from time to time we do get a group of people who turn up because they are not happy about something. The board needs to know why. The meetings provide a first-class early warning system, and act as a safety valve preventing issues from getting out of perspective. I would be unhappy to see them disappear. Indeed, it is a system to be recommended to other employee-focused businesses. There is really no substitute for being able to question the boss.

The centrepiece of our shareholder involvement programme is our annual general meeting. It is there that we take the really big policy issues collectively. We want our shareholders to be present, but we do not want them to be there when they should be working. So our AGMs are always on a Saturday or Sunday. We arrange free transport to the venue and we provide them with lunch after the meeting is over. We *do not* pay them to be there, and if they require overnight accommodation they must pay for it themselves. The issues that we have put to them, and that they have decided over the years, are the fundamental policies which have determined the future of the NFC. Some of the issues decided are as follows:

> Who will serve on the board? Every director tells me that standing up and facing the employee shareholders as they vote on whether he should be on the board is an anxious moment. From time to time investors have made it plain that they wish to protest against a particular director by voting against his election.

> What kind of board shall we have? The shareholders voted in favour of a shareholder director elected by one man, one vote. They were against an employee director elected by one employee, one vote. I was personally in favour of an employee director; the board was split on the issue and the shareholders decided it for us. They argued that the shareholders already had a special board

member – all an employee had to do if he wanted special representation was to buy shares. They overwhelmingly did not want a trade union representative on the board.

Fifteen per cent of pre-tax profit should be allocated for profit-sharing to ensure that the new generation of employees could obtain a worthwhile capital stake in the business.

One per cent of the shares of the company should be allocated to a trust to look after hardship cases among former employees.

One per cent of pre-tax profits should be given to charities of their choice each year.

A partially elected council should be set up to supervise NFC Social Responsibilities.

It can be argued that these last four decisions have reduced in the short term the market value of NFC by about £150m. But the shareholders know in the long term that these decisions will create a better company, which will show better returns, than a company that does not have these values.

The company should seek to have its shares listed on the Stock Exchange, but only if particular safeguards are in place to preserve the uniqueness of NFC as a company.

Through the process of consultation outside the AGM but through specially arranged meetings, they helped formulate and endorse the strategic direction of the business they owned.

If you coupled these policy decisions with the close questioning of the board on the annual accounts, it is hard to imagine how those of the shareholders who wish to be involved could be more involved. It may be true that those who are active are the minority, but in any human activity it was ever thus. Success does tend to lead to inertia – 'The Board know what they are doing so why should we bother?' However, if things go wrong, that is the time that any board needs detailed questioning, and, if the problems are outside their making, needs support. I believe our well-established system of shareholder involvement will ensure that this will happen – not that any of us are actively seeking to try it out!

The AGMs are social as well as business events. The atmosphere outside the meetings is like a family party. We encourage this. Every other year we try and make a weekend of it by going to a seaside resort (often Blackpool), organizing dances for the pensioners, parties for the kids and a music hall for everyone the previous day. The board have even been known to reveal their thespian ambitions – the verdict is that they should stick to running the business!

At the end of the AGM we want people to depart feeling that they have been involved in a professionally presented business session. They have taken part in the debate and have voted on the key problems facing the business. They have had a good time and can go back to their work places determined to play their part in continuing NFC's success.

Some say it is all a charade. Rarely if ever are the board's recommendations thrown out. It is not, therefore, a business that is influenced or controlled by its employees. My answer is simple. Firstly, you can see by the mission statements how much senior management have changed their way of running the business as a result of being accountable to their employees as shareholders. Secondly, each shareholder is given the opportunity and is encouraged to be involved. If we as leaders persuade them that our way forward is the best, this does not deny their involvement. If they believe that it is *their* business and that they want to work for its success, surely that is what share ownership as a motivator is all about. Pride of ownership is a state of mind.

Is it Successful?

'We had a vision . . .'
The Times, 19 January 1982

'A beautifully run company with an aggressively competitive management which exem-
plifies the power of the "nice" strategy.'
Financial Weekly, 23 February 1989

Success can be measured in many ways. The simplistic businessman will aver that it is all about the 'bottom line'. Only if earnings
per share or profit before tax are progressive can a company
claim to be successful. But surely this is the lowest hurdle that
has to be jumped, the necessary minimum objective? A company
that can only claim profitability cannot claim total success. There
are many other criteria that have to be met before real success
emerges. Growth of employment opportunities; a satisfied, productive, well-paid, trained and happy staff; the company playing
a full role in the community and meeting its moral responsibilities
to society. These are the important values to the great companies
of the world.

We did realize, though, that no one would take seriously our
experiment in employee ownership unless it was profitable, not
only profitable, but it had to be demonstrably more profitable
and more dynamic than its competitors. There is little doubt that
so far it has met this minimum hurdle. For six years NFC has
achieved compound growth in profits before tax in excess of 40
per cent per annum, and growth in earnings per share in excess
of 30 per cent.

It is relatively easy for a company to increase pre-tax profits.

It can do this by acquiring companies and issuing its own shares as the means of purchase. The real test is whether, in making acquisitional and organic growth, a company is pushing its earnings per share along at a pace to match its growth in pre-tax profits. Many companies on the surface do a good job when only profit growth is highlighted. There are fewer that pass the ultimate test that earnings per share grow at the same pace. NFC has issued very few new shares in its seven-year life. Up to the time of flotation the number of new shares issued had only been 6 per cent. All of these had been issued to employees or trading partners. To issue new shares would have resulted in a dilution of 'family' ownership, as it was unlikely that the family shareholders could have found the additional money to take up the new shares if there had been a stream of rights issues. The new shares would inevitably have found their way into the hands of the institutions, thus diluting employee ownership. Our mission statement is unequivocal – we seek to maintain employee control. Since we have issued no shares for acquisitions, the geometric increase in profits before tax has fed straight into earnings per share. In part this focus upon the importance of earnings per share has caused the astronomical rise in the capital value of the employees' shares.

Our shareholders well understand how shares are valued. The share price is the rating that the stock market gives to a company expressed as the number of times a buyer is prepared to pay now for each year's earnings per share. Historic growth of earnings per share is what gives the shrewd investor most insight into the strength of a company. Earnings per share, therefore, is for us the king of all the ratios by which we judge our business – increasingly senior management bonusing depends on it.

Driven by two strong forces – maintaining employee control which limits the issue of new shares, and the growth of share value, NFC has concentrated on pushing earnings per share. I cannot remember the board ever taking a major decision which would have prejudiced the growth in earnings per share. But neither have I been conscious that NFC has sacrificed the long term for the short term, which is the usual accusation levelled at the companies whose god is EPS. I assume that the aim of most companies is to survive and stay independent. If this is the principal objective, it is too risky a strategy to offer the shareholders profit jam tomorrow. Jam tomorrow is not what most owners want – whether they are employees, private individuals or financial institutions. It is no good complaining that owners should not be like that – they have their own pressures. In the main they invest in a company because they seek a combination of fair dividends and good capital growth. A jam-tomorrow approach to earnings per share makes a company's shares less attractive to the average investor and hence the value of the shares drops. A low market rating in turn makes the company vulnerable to a takeover, and hence it risks its independent survival.

The stakes in this game have always been too high for me to want to play. We have therefore made sure that our annual investment decisions taken together do not *plan* a reduction in earnings per share. If a reduction happens because of the unforeseen collapse of the market, that is another matter. Focusing on the progressive growth of earnings per share does not predicate inadequate investment for the future. It merely means that management has to get the right balance in its allocation of resources between those projects which produce profit today and those that are about profit tomorrow.

Neither am I persuaded by the argument that a particular strategic acquisition must be made because it is the last chance available to complete a market domination or growth strategy. The acquisition must consequently be grabbed at a crazily high price, even if that price depresses earnings per share for two or three years. The basis of such argument is that this is the last bus to town so we had better catch it today. I have learnt that another bus is usually coming along tomorrow. Our progress had perforce to be to plan growth using the cash we generated and any further borrowings that we could arrange within our bank covenants, not to issue new shares.

Has the vision and supporting strategy worked out in practice? Our first strategy of debt reduction – which was a normal knee-jerk reaction to our mountain of debt – soon lost its flavour. Within twelve months the board had to decide whether to hold business growth back by continuing its policy of cash starvation, or to recognize that down the line the motivational change which

139

we had hoped for was actually taking place. The companies were beginning to win significant slugs of new business. It did not take the board long to change tack and to recognize that we had to support our management's market successes. This meant an end to our debt reduction phase. We had to find ways of financing the new business.

Bankers are a funny lot. They insisted upon stringent covenants when they lent us the money to buy the company. Hardly was the ink dry on the loan agreement when, not as a syndicate, but as individual banks, they were presenting us with a whole series of financing schemes that effectively evaded the barbed wire of the covenant fences that they had just collectively erected. The schemes could all be classified under the global heading of 'off balance sheet financing'. The extensive use of off balance sheet finance caught the eye of the accountancy profession, and they are now busy issuing new rules to bring off balance sheet debt back into the open and on to the balance sheet.

The financial world is like a game of cops and robbers, the robbers being the high-paid corporate advisers who spend their time designing intricate financial and tax schemes to evade accountancy rules. The accountancy profession are the ponderous cops trying to arrest the progress of the robbers. It is all a happy, expensive, non-productive game because at the end of the day it does not make any real difference to the underlying strength of a company whether the borrowings are on or off balance sheet. All it needs is for the banks and other finance businesses to take a more rational approach to lending. They should lend not on assets – and balance sheet strength – but to good management, and seek their comfort from the cash generation of the business. It is not usually the sale of assets that pays the interest and reduces the loan, it is the normal cash flow of the company. But the cops and robbers game will continue – it is far too lucrative in fees for both the cops and the robbers for them ever to want to give it up.

Having been shown how to play the debt-financing game by rules acceptable to the City, we made sure that we were professionals at it. Over the years we have raised many millions of off balance sheet finance to fund the new business that our managers were winning. It gives some measure of our willingness to support success to compare capital investment when we were state-owned to what it has become under the 'new' ownership. The government, during the seven years I was Chief Executive, never approved capital expenditure of more than £25m in any year. Annually since 1985 we have invested over £200m a year on new vehicles, depots, computer systems, travel shops and acquisitions. The fact that we financed a large part of this in the early days by various non-recourse, off balance sheet and operational leasing schemes is irrelevant. In our business today's capital expenditure is tomorrow's profit and cash flow. As we have become more profitable so we have been able to finance more and more of our capital expenditure from our own re- sources. But we needed the guts to move out of a debt-reduction frame of mind into the attitude of 'let's get out there and take the opportunities that a newly motivated workforce are generating'. This happened despite our accountancy-led past where somehow reducing interest payments on debt seemed safer than investing in new projects in the hope of getting future profits.

This represented another milestone in the process of manage- ment at the top changing its attitudes. It must not be forgotten that the management running the new NFC was the same as had run the old NFC. For ten years, from 1972–82, we had been 'accountant dominated'. The task was to get the cost line below the revenue line. While doing this we reduced the workforce from 51,700 to 23,000. Yet here were the same people being bold enough to take the risks involved of aggressively gearing up the debt of the business, hoping that we would be able to make the revenue line overtake a rising cost line. In this way the profit which had eluded us when we were accountant led would, we hoped, flow through now we were market led.

Many business theorists have postulated that there are two kinds of manager – the cost cutter and the marketeer. No man- ager is good at both, they say. Therefore, depending upon the analysis of the problem, a business in football terms needs either a clogger or a striker. NFC has demonstrated that the same management team given a different culture in which to manage can change themselves from being defenders into attackers.

Part of our vision was to be the market leaders in the UK in contract hire and distribution. There is little doubt that the change of ownership helped this strategy. It was incredibly difficult to sell these services to private industry when we were state-owned. They looked upon most state industries as being anything but service-orientated. Who could say they were wrong, when they were suffering at the hands of the state-owned telephone, postal, gas and electricity services? I remember how many chief executives' eyes used to cloud over when I was pitching to take over their in-house vehicle fleets, and I tried to persuade them that NFC, although nationalized, was really a high customer service business. With the change of ownership we had something positive to sell. 'The driver who delivers your goods, sir, to your customers will be certain to give good service because his own money is at stake if he doesn't.' It was and still is an attractive selling message.

So our core business of transport and distribution started to flourish. Perversely they were helped by the recession in the UK of 1981–83. In considering their strategies for survival, companies were taken by the need to concentrate on their own core activities. Was operation of the logistics chain really a core activity to most businesses? Our marketing message was that while every business had to 'control' their own logistics and distribution operations, i.e., they had to specify the service levels and monitor the performance, they could control it without investing in it valuable capital and key management. There was no need for them actually to operate their logistic system. Logistics was an entirely separate business needing different management skills to retailing or manufacturing. As we were able to show success in operating services for leading companies like Sainsbury's and Marks & Spencer's, the tide in favour of contracting out the logistics operations began to flow in our favour.

Unilever decided to move out of its own distribution so we were able to take over SPD, one of the largest and most respected operators in this field. A year or two later Birds Eye Walls sold to us their cold stores and vehicles, as did Lyons Maid and Findus. We built new purpose-designed distribution centres for many customers, with whom deals were always backed by the long-term commitment that we would be their distribution operator for five to ten years. We took over many large transport fleets –

and because we could improve efficiency we were able to show significant cost savings. So the vision of being market leaders in transport and distribution in the UK was fulfilled.

Another part of the vision was to develop a worldwide household removals business. In the early part of the century it was emigrants, seeking to find a new life in the USA, Canada, Australia, New Zealand, who were the major people moving home from one country to another. They took what goods and chattels they could with them, but in the main their possessions were small in value and size. In the last two decades we have seen the growth of a more affluent group of people moving their homes internationally. Commerce and industry has become global. Consumer taste has become more global – witness worldwide the success of Coca-Cola, McDonalds, Kentucky Fried Chicken. Who would have believed the Chinese would eat Kentucky Fried Chicken and wash it down with Coke when it costs them an average of one week's wages to enjoy this repast? Retailing, which was never believed to be exportable, is showing signs of global expansion. Global financial services are needed to support worldwide service and manufacturing industry. We saw that all this would mean that there would be more businessmen moving from their own countries to manage the overseas operations of the international companies.

Executives were a very different breed to emigrants. They were affluent, with a plethora of personal household possessions which they wanted to have around them in their new environments. What to take and what not to take would not be a cost-sensitive decision because in the main their companies would be paying the bill. But which removals company to use would be very service-sensitive. They would demand that their prized possessions were not damaged in transit, and were delivered on time.

In the 1970s almost all international removals were done by using overseas agents. So Pickfords in the UK would quote for moving household effects to the USA. They would pack, load and ship and then give it to one of their US agents to deliver, unload and unpack. It was difficult, if not impossible, to guarantee a constant quality of service throughout. We decided we would create a unique selling proposition (which is what all

143

marketeers are seeking) if we could claim 'Pickfords collects – Pickfords unloads at your overseas destination wherever it is in the civilized world'.

To do this we had to create a worldwide network of household removals companies which were owned and controlled by Pickfords. This was our vision. We started to test the theory by buying a bankrupt removals company in Australia. The volume of the business we did between the UK and Australia increased significantly. Next we set up Pickfords operations in Hong Kong, Singapore and New Zealand. The small network was shown to work.

The largest executive moving market was the USA. We knew we had to get a presence there. Our first attempt to enter the USA was when we took an option to buy a company which was clearly in difficulties. It was, I believe, the 'last bus' syndrome that drove us to contemplate taking on this company. Ted Wall, our International Director, had been trying to get a foothold in the US for some three years and, despite contacting every removals van-line, had had no success. To take on the ailing business seemed to be our last bus to town. It was a mistake. We did not take up the option when, after a few weeks of being close to the company, we saw the real difficulties that it faced. Our withdrawal attracted much adverse criticism and, as is inevitable in the States, not an inconsiderable number of legal actions.

Within four months came the opportunity out of the blue of bidding for the No. 1 removals company in the USA – Allied Van Lines. Since its inception over sixty years ago Allied had been an agents' cooperative. We never believed that the agents who had banded themselves together to offer a nationwide branded removals service to the citizens of the USA would ever decide to sell their cooperative to a third party – particularly a third party from the UK. However, the seven hundred agents in every major US city recognized that if they were to compete successfully in their domestic transport market, which was being deregulated, they had to be able to take decisions more quickly and more commercially than could be done by a cooperative.

It was the most complex takeover I had ever witnessed, and it was our employee-focused values that helped us to win. For the members of the Allied Cooperative, it was an easier step to sell to a business owned by its employees than to sell to a normal company. But first of all we had to bid an acceptable price so that the merchant bank and the special committee of the agents evaluating the bids could recommend the price. We knew that the only thing of value that we were buying was the commitment of the agents to use the Interstate Van Line services in the future. It would be no good for us to buy the agents' shares and then for them to take the money and give their business to the opposition. So our offer was conditional upon at least 80 per cent of the agents being prepared to sign a long-term (five-year) contract to continue to be Allied agents.

At the start of our campaign to persuade the agents that NFC was the right partner for them, one of their senior agents said to me, 'In the whole history of Allied Van Lines we have *never* had 80 per cent of these independent businessmen all pointing in the same direction.' So across the US, in five separate major presentations, a team led by Ted Wall presented NFC and its values to the seven hundred agents. In American terms it was a dog and pony show. In our terms it was an attempt, using our communicating skills, our knowledge, our business values, but above all our humour, to convince them that the new partnership would give them the commercial bite which the old cooperative arrangements had failed to do.

Denis Olliver, now Managing Director of the worldwide Home Services division, used to finish the presentation by saying, 'If we haven't been able to persuade you by now that we can bring new drive and profitability to your business, the only other thing we can offer you is virility. We have a sixty-year-old Chairman with a six-month-old baby!' By this time I had remarried and was lucky enough to have started a second family with my new wife Lydia.

We will never know whether it was the offer of virility or the quality of our future business mission that finally persuaded 99 per cent of the agents to accept the deal, and to sign the long-term contracts committing their interstate removals business to the Van Line for the next five years.

So we now had the US covered. In the next year or two we will have household removal companies in Canada and all the major European countries. Already we have put together the most global household removals business in the world and we are well on the way to realizing the vision contained in the 1983 strategic review.

The development of the worldwide removals service was part of the wider strategy we had for internationalizing NFC. If we were to become a 'company for all seasons', with the innate strength to resist economic downturn, a significant part of our profits had to be earned in countries other than the UK. We had to be less dependent upon the poorly performing and unreliable UK economy. That was certainly true of the 1970s – although in the last four years the UK economy has performed well and has shown above average growth.

We set ourselves in 1982 the target of having 25 per cent of our profits coming from outside the UK by 1990. There was no magic in the number. Starting from nothing and bearing in mind the level of on balance sheet debt we could afford, it seemed a target that with a fair wind we might just achieve. The easiest way to get a foothold into other countries was by making an acquisition. This was preferable to the long haul of starting from a green field site. But it was not possible – or at least we did not find a way – to buy companies except by raising debt on the balance sheet. So we had to use the very scarce 'on balance sheet' debt allowed to us by the banks' covenants for these acquisitions.

The full brunt of developing overseas fell on Ted Wall, our International Director. He was another Yorkshireman, of great tenacity and with excellent negotiating skills. He was an extrovert with a large fund of good humour. His job was to organize the research into which of our UK services we should expand overseas; then to identify the particular target company; to negotiate the acquisition, and, when it was acquired, to manage it and supervise its organic growth.

The first acquisition in Australia in 1981/82 – just at the time of the buy-out – was a dog. We had tried to get into Australia over the previous eighteen months but had found problems because of the then attitude of the Australian government. They were concerned that too much of their business was owned by overseas companies. Their policy was to try to 'buy back the farm'. So they were reluctant to allow any Australian company to have a majority of its shares acquired by an overseas company, unless there were compelling research or technology gains. This was before the new band of Australian entrepreneurs set forth to pillage the world. Bond, Packer, Murdoch, Elliott and Abells proved in the 1980s to be as formidable a pack of overseas acquirers as any country could field.

We heard that Downards, an old, established Melbourne-based transport company, was in the hands of the receivers. We bid for the company and were successful, subject to government approval. The transport industry in Australia did not want us there and they lobbied powerfully in Canberra against our being allowed to acquire the company. The only weapon Ted Wall had with the Labour Minister of Transport was that if NFC bought the company, some four hundred jobs would be saved. This argument was persuasive and on Christmas Eve 1981 we were given the go ahead.

Our investment policy for overseas acquisitions was in shreds. We should only have been buying a profitable company with good management. However, needs must if the devil drives and we knew we would not be able to buy such a company in Australia. If we wished to be there we had to go in via a bankrupt company. Downards management needed to be remotivated, and it proved to be a long haul to turn the company around. It is *not* a sensible way of entering a new country.

In the meantime, Ted Wall went to the USA and targeted for acquisition a transport company, which provided delivery services to the home, based in California. He did a deal with the owner, who was ill with heart problems, to buy the company subject to a 'due diligence' audit. We sent a team out to evaluate the company and to produce a plan to improve profits which would justify the purchase price. They produced a good plan and recommended the purchase at a price of around $14m. But by now we were in the final throes of completing the buy-out of NFC. We could not take on more debt, and had to decline the purchase. The owner of the business was impressed with the manager we sent to lead the evaluation team and also with the plan he proposed for improving it. He offered our man a job as general manager which he accepted. So we lost the business and lost a very good manager!

147

However, that was not the end of it. We kept in touch, and three years later we bought the business from the executors of the owner's will. The business had been improved and many of the NFC systems and values incorporated. Nevertheless, it did cost us an extra $5m. So Merchants Home Delivery Service came into NFC after over four years of stalking. It has been a good acquisition with the volume of its business having grown out of all recognition since coming into the NFC family.

The other strategic thrust was in the logistics field. We had targeted Home Services & Logistics as being the services which we would give priority to developing overseas. Ted Wall, following commissioned research, spoke to the owner of a business that had the qualities we were looking for. The company was Dauphin Distribution Services based in the small Pennsylvania town of Mechanicsburg. It had been built up from scratch by a marvellously earthy character, Jim Adams. He was approaching sixty and Ted Wall's phone call made him think about the future; whether it was time to realize some of the value in his business and contemplate retirement in a year or two. He and Ted Wall got on well immediately. Although he wanted a fair price, Jim Adams was a man who had his employees, who had helped him to build the company, very much in mind. The NFC philosophy of employee involvement and share ownership appealed to him, and without seeking any other bidder he did the deal direct with Ted Wall. Dauphin is now a respected and growing member of the NFC logistics group.

The acquisition actively demonstrated to me that employee ownership and people-focused policies are not only attractive to employees and customers, but also to owners who had built companies themselves and who, when it came to selling, wanted to ensure a good future for their own employees. In our three major acquisitions in the USA – Merchants, Allied Van Lines and Dauphin – these factors played a part. When we took over SPD in the UK, Unilever were also insistent that the company should be transferred only to a buyer who would respect the employment rights of their employees.

By the end of 1988 some 23 per cent of NFC's profits were now earned overseas. We look set to achieve the 25 per cent by the end of 1990. This is a clear example of a visionary target set seven years ago that with our financing constraints seemed to be almost impossible, and yet it will be achieved. NFC is a stronger company for it.

I must not give the impression that all of our strategic targets were met. We had a bad failure with the vision we had to build a successful computer software company. Like many large companies we had an in-house computer company. The management presented a picture of burgeoning growth in information technology over the next decade. It impressed the strategy working party and we could see no good reason why they should not break out of their in-house focus and sell their software programs to the world. We underestimated the cultural change, and how much the management had to be improved to penetrate the competitive outside market. We learnt the lesson the hard way that a peripheral activity is unlikely to have the necessary depth of corporate management strength to make it a success, when compared with the skills of the entrepreneurs who prosper without the backing of a captive in-house customer. Why we had to learn that lesson, I will never know. After all, it was the sales pitch we gave to our potential customers who were running in-house distribution and transport operations. After three years of dismal attempts to penetrate the external IT market, we gave up and recognized that this was an area where our ambitions outweighed our abilities.

Property development and travel were two other services which were not strictly core products, but which our strategy review decided could grow if we were prepared to allocate to them the necessary management and capital. We have made a fair fist of both. Pickfords Travel now has over four hundred retail and business shops. It is the third largest travel retailer in the UK. Its profits have grown in five out of seven years, and it is now expanding its activities overseas. It is very much a people's business. The way the travel clerk greets the customer and deals with his needs gives marketing edge. We believe still that in the long run our people values will give us the advantage over our competitors. It is going to be much tougher than we had imagined, but if the market is set fair (travel will become the largest industry in the world by the end of the century – larger even than agriculture), and you believe that you have a formula that will give you marketing advantage, persistence is vital. It is a mistake constantly to be changing strategic direction if the fundamentals are right – even if the bottom-line profit is variable. Stick with it – but be sure the fundamentals are right.

Property development was almost thrust upon us. We acquired a land bank which with the UK property boom of the 1980s has proved to be more valuable than anyone imagined. We brought in the skills, not just to sell sites – which was all that we were allowed to do when we were state owned – but to develop them. In future we would act as the property developer. We have made increasing profits out of this activity. First, we developed only our own sites which is relatively risk free. Latterly, we have been buying sites and developing them. This raises the risk profile. We are partners in the development of the largest and potentially most exciting urban regeneration site in Europe – the 110 acres around King's Cross Station in London. We also own some 20 per cent of the land. We inherited the advantage of a first-class land bank.

Yet I have always had a nagging doubt as to whether this is really our world. Our central skill is running service companies which employ many people, whom we know how to involve and motivate. Property development is about a few talented, self-motivated individuals entrepreneurially grabbing opportunities and fixing deals. It does not fit conceptually into NFC's central strength. But after much debate, it was given development status. It has done well. It has always met its targets and has contributed in full to the realization of the vision of the future. But the nagging doubt has remained with me, though not, I hastily add, with my colleagues.

So today the NFC is stronger financially and has a broader product base. It has extended its wings overseas and is much better able to resist economic cycles. It is people focused and continues to have vision. It has increased its operating profits at an average annual growth rate in excess of 40 per cent, and earnings per share have similarly escalated. It is out-performing its competitors in nearly every market it is in, and it has the highest stock market rating of any large company in the transport sector in the UK. I believe in strict business terms we can claim success.

But there are wider considerations. Full success demands positive answers to more fundamental questions. Has the company offered increased employment opportunities? Has it a satisfied, productive and well-paid staff? Is the company playing its full role in the community? Are we meeting our responsibilities to society? The answers to these questions cannot be quantified, hence my evaluation has to be more subjective.

We now employ in excess of 33,000 people worldwide and the numbers are rising. We only had 23,000 on the payroll in 1982 – and the numbers were falling. So the number of jobs available is now some 40 per cent higher, and, without doubt, the quality, interest and skill requirements of the jobs have improved.

A young man joining NFC today and willing to climb the tree must have a far wider range of skills. He must understand the full range of expertise that is required by the logistics function, and, in addition, he should have international experience. So employment in quality and quantity has been enhanced. The evidence shows also that people of real calibre are moving up the promotion mountain at a faster pace. As an example, the last two appointees to the main board were in their late thirties, a full decade younger than the last generation of board promotions.

This accelerated career progression can cause problems for the prospects of the next generation because it will be fifteen to twenty years before these new board appointees are due to retire. Hence, promotion to the board will be blocked unless the earlier retirement of existing board members is encouraged. I believe the retirement age for management will get progressively younger – within ten years I can imagine senior managers leaving at the age of fifty-five, perhaps to start a new, less demanding business career. In the case of NFC, we should have been able to provide them with enough capital through profit-sharing and share ownership to enable them to have the money to form their own business – or, indeed, the wherewithal to go off and live on a desert island. The days of one job, one company from age eighteen to sixty-five are over. We should recognize this and facilitate it. In its turn it will mean that large companies will be being run by people in the prime of their life, which, for properly-trained businessmen, I would judge to be in their mid-forties. At this age the experience is there, the energy is there, and the executive is not playing the business bowling from memory. They will not be suffering from business *déjà vu*, i.e., dismissing ideas simply because they have been tried before. There are surprisingly few new ideas in the business world, but an old idea at the right time psychologically, can be more effective than a new idea introduced when the time is not ripe.

I do think, therefore, that we have fulfilled the part of the mission statement which required us to increase employment opportunities. Are our employees more satisfied? How do you define satisfaction? For sure they don't leave the company as frequently as before – labour turnover has declined – but some will argue that this is brought about by increased unemployment and is general to all UK companies. They do attend work more regularly and we have less absenteeism. But again, you can argue that this is a feature of an expanding workforce with a lower average age. An employee in his mid-twenties will tend to have more commitments, in the way of children to educate, mortgage to pay, mouths to feed, and hence he is less likely to take time off as he doesn't wish to suffer a reduction in take-home pay. He also tends to be fitter than a sixty-year-old.

Satisfaction should manifest itself in less industrial stoppages, walk-outs and working to rule. Certainly this has been the case. We have had no significant stoppage in the last eight years. Furthermore, there have been some quite remarkable examples of employee loyalty. One example concerns the distribution operation we do for a major brewer in the south-east. The customer had a militant workforce in the brewery. Over the years there were many stoppages. The production workers were in the same union lodge as the distribution drivers. Whenever the production workers withdrew their labour, they invariably prevailed upon the distribution drivers to support their stoppage. This meant that the strike was quickly effective, no beer was brewed and within a short space of time the pubs and clubs were out of stock because there was no distribution system. About nine months after the NFC took over the distribution operations, the production workers went on strike. They immediately picketed our two distribution depots.

The drivers who were now NFC men went through the pickets for the first five days – a thing unheard of in previous disputes. They then said to us, 'You have the legal means available to remove the secondary picketing. You get them off the gate by the weekend.' This we did by taking out the first labour injunction in our history. So the production workers' strike was ineffective as supplies were able to be brought in by our people from other breweries. You may suggest that this was brought about by the new industrial relations legislation of the Thatcher government. I think there was more to it than that.

Another outstanding example of people's preference for staying in work rather than walking through the gates was over the merging of the two parcel companies. Despite union calls for days of protest and the withdrawal of labour, not one single productive hour was lost.

Employee loyalty was again demonstrated when we decided that we were unlikely to be a big player in the waste management industry. We had a relatively small company based in the north-west, and at the time we did not have the capital available to make the investment for it to become a force in this growing industry. The senior management of the business felt that if we could not afford to develop the business, the company and the employees would have a better future as part of a larger group whose main purpose was to be at the forefront of the emerging technology of dealing with waste in all its forms. We received a bid from such a company. At the time we were desperately short of cash and we were tempted to sell. But remembering our beliefs in participative management and the right of the individual to have a say in the decisions which affect his life, we told the company management to sound out the views of the employees. We also made available £1m of the potential purchase price to be distributed amongst the staff as a kind of farewell present. Admittedly, the would-be purchasers did not make much of a presentation to our staff to encourage them to join the new group. For whatever reason, on a vote, 98 per cent said that they would prefer to stay with the NFC. They even went so far as to say they valued our management style. Faced with this reaction from the employees, the board took the decision not to sell.

There is enough anecdotal and real evidence to suggest that

153

employees are more satisfied. They are more willing to come to work, and work more effectively when they are there.

By contrast we have deliberately sought to encourage their constructive dissatisfaction. We do not want a compliant workforce. We want a workforce that is dissatisfied with the way things are being done, and is confident enough to raise that dissatisfaction in a positive way. Every week I get letters from employees asking why we are not doing things which would improve our service to customers. At company level there is an increased willingness to criticize existing standards of service. At the top level of the business I get the feeling that if I decide we should do something, it is never regarded as an instruction, merely as the start of a debate! This is what our participative management style is all about.

We also have evidence from two of the MORI attitude surveys we did in 1982 and again in 1988 which suggests that the employees are becoming more satisfied with the way the business is being managed. I cannot *prove* greater satisfaction among the employees, but surely, as Dudley Moore might say to Peter Cook, 'It's bleeding obvious, Pete.' If people are treated as individuals, their views are sought and respected, their rights are enhanced and they share in the wealth they are creating, it must lead to more satisfaction at the workplace. If it doesn't, I must confess I don't know what does.

Have we a better-trained, more productive workforce? The statistics show that we are more productive. This can only be measured across a diverse business like NFC by how much turnover and profit per employee have increased, which have grown before adjustment for inflation by 93 per cent and 201 per cent over the six years.

Whether everyone is better trained is more difficult to assess. Better trained if measured by the number of training days per annum per employee, but we are lagging behind our Japanese and European competitors (who isn't?). This is something that we are addressing – the sheer quantum of on- and off-job training will go up and is going up each year. But we have a mountain to climb to be a world-class player in training when measured quantitatively.

Most UK companies have the same problem. The lack of

training by world standards in the UK is at last getting the attention it deserves. British management now recognizes that in order to have a product and marketing edge over international competitors, a trained workforce is a prerequisite. With increasing profitability business is prepared to make the investment. The campaign is gaining momentum with new initiatives in both vocational and skills training coming from government. In addition, there are signs that the basic educational system in the UK is changing its bias against industry, and business is working much harder with the schools to ensure this trend continues. But industrialists, educationalists and government have much work to do together if we are to have the trained workforce to match our international competitors. In the meantime, NFC will be doing its bit by increasing the quality and volume of our general skills and management training.

We are proud of our management training programme which takes on increasing numbers of graduates each year. Initially, NFC gives them formal training in business skills, while the companies provide them with early opportunities to run their own small operations – depots, travel shops, warehouses – within the discipline of a profit and loss account. We believe we are lucky to be able to offer this type of early appointment to graduates. Responsibility and accountability is what the good young manager wants – we are able to provide this. We do not have a system that mollycoddles the potential crown prince. After his initial year's formal training, the graduate has to find his own way upwards within his company. One of the qualities we are looking for in top management is the ability to find answers to increasingly more complex business problems. If a high flyer can't find his way, almost unaided, through the problem of his own self-development, he has not demonstrated all the qualities we seek at the top. We try to create the environment where there is opportunity for advancement, but self-motivation is all important in taking the opportunity. Youngsters will be counselled and appraised as are all our staff, but after the initial training they will be encouraged to find their own way through. Some ten years later – if they really are high flyers – they may begin to come to the attention of the centre again. The manpower reviews which are part of the planning system should identify within five years those who are capable of being company managing directors or functional directors – those capable of filling one of the top hundred jobs in the NFC.

At this stage we try to ensure that the individual does receive as broad a business experience as possible. This may mean serving overseas, moving from one division to another, having an external mid-career course at an international business school, or simply being picked out to tackle an intractable business problem. These young high flyers *are* our future. NFC controls the allocation of this resource in the same way that it controls the allocation of capital – except that good management is scarcer and more precious than capital in this day and age of free credit. The training and development of young people is vital and we can never spend enough time and creativity in ensuring its success.

Let me now turn to pay. Do we 'pay' our staff well? We have never used the stock ownership plan to ask our employees to work at lower than industry wage levels. In the USA there have been many examples of companies which, after getting into difficulties, invite their employees to take wage cuts to help the company through the trouble. In exchange the employees are given an equity stake in the business. We have never had to do this. We recognize our employment package must be more than competitive as our future success depends upon having a workforce that is of above average quality. As far as basic rates and overtime are concerned, we pay the industry average (re-membering that we are in more than one industry – for example, car transport drivers and oil tanker drivers have always been more highly paid than delivery drivers). In addition we tend to have better fringe benefits – such as pensions and sickness pay. We have larger productivity incentive payments which depend upon individual performance, and we have the profit-sharing scheme. This is payable either in cash, which is not tax effective, or in shares in NFC, which is tax effective. The quantum of profit-sharing depends on NFC improving year after year its earnings per share. In 1988/89 the average payments from profit-sharing will be about £600, which will be around 5 per cent of an individual's gross pay. But this will only be paid if earnings per share before profit-sharing increase year on year by at least 20 per cent. So we are competitive in the package we offer our manual grades, and compared with our competitors we offer a more balanced reward package than merely going for money up front.

Managers and senior managers must be well remunerated if we are to keep ahead of the competition. However, we have had to earn the right to be high payers. When, back in 1982, we were a low-performing company, we related our senior management salaries to those being paid by the lower quartile of British companies. As we have worked up the performance league, so we have moved our salary policy to the point where we now pay in line with the upper quartile of British business. Upper quartile pay for upper quartile performance. In addition, senior management salaries are heavily performance-related – bonus, merit reviews and profit-sharing all have a significant part to play in the total package.

We are not paternalistic; we do not give fringe benefits, we prefer to give cash and let the individual decide for himself what he wants to spend it on. The exception is if there are clear tax advantages. So we do give cars and good pensions which are tax effective to the individual, but we do not provide private health cover which has no tax relief at present. We have never given share options. With our philosophy, we would have to offer the options not to a select few but to the whole workforce. We know they are a general feature of the top executive package in most industries and our package has to be competitive. However, I believe that share options have nothing like the motivational effect of profit-sharing in shares.

With share options there are no downside risks – the executive does not lose everything that he has ever had if at the end of the five-year option period the shares have declined in value. He has not, during those five years, become an actual shareholder in the company. He has no right to vote his shares on important company issues. He has received no dividends and he has not shared in the wealth he is creating. There is no real evidence that at the end of the option period the executives use their options to build significant real stakes in their companies. They usually have to sell the major portion of the options they have been granted to pay the option price of the shares. It is not unusual, at the end of the option period, for an executive's

157

options to be topped up again to take into account the options that he has sold. So options are used as a way of paying three- or five-year bonuses to management. They do not effectively ensure that an executive has a long-term stake in the company and hence has greater commitment to the success of the business.

None of these criticisms can be levelled at our profit-sharing schemes. Any shares that are awarded become the 'property' of the individual immediately, but are held in trust for tax purposes for five years. He has the right to vote the shares, the right to dividends, and, if he wishes to forgo the tax advantages, the right to sell and realize the capital. If he wants to invest some of his earnings and buy extra shares he can do so, and be rewarded by one extra free share for every three he saves for. Again, the shares become his possession immediately. If the purpose is to spread wider share ownership, this second part of our scheme must be better than the normal save-as-you-earn scheme. Under these schemes an option price is given at which the employee can buy shares five years later. His savings are put into a building society and at the end of five years the employee decides whether to spend the savings on other things or take up shares at the option price. There is no risk. It must be a greater incentive for an individual to see that his actions at work can affect the value of the capital that he has sunk into the business. We have therefore turned our back on options as a milk-and-water approach to employee capitalism. They are better than nothing, but are not in the same league as profit-sharing and bonus shares for saving.

When NFC came to the stock market we were even able to convince the hard-nosed City analysts and investors that profit-sharing is a better motivational tool than share options. I suspect that profit-sharing in shares got a bad reputation because of the scheme ICI introduced in the 1950s. Here the employee was obliged to accept shares if the company had a good year, whether he wanted them or not. So stories emerged about stockbrokers being outside the gates of the major ICI factories buying the employees' shares for cash as soon as they were issued. We felt this debased the concept. We have learnt from this. We give each employee the choice – he can have money or shares. If, as 90 per cent do, shares are chosen, there is a fair chance that the employee will retain the shares and leave his capital stake in the company. This will be reinforced if the company goes out of its way to make sure that its employee shareholders are treated as special people, whose opinions on the future of the business are welcomed.

Perhaps the last yardstick by which the better companies are measured is their attitude towards the community in which they do business. It can be argued that it is not the role of business to be involved with charity, with the aged, with community projects, with sport and particularly with the support of the arts. For example, two or three years after the buy-out, I proposed to the NFC board that in recognition of the good fortune we were all experiencing we should give half of our final dividend to charity; at the same time, that we should let it be known that we expected this of others. This proposal met with little support. The predominant view was that charity was a personal matter and that the board should not seek to influence an individual's charitable activities. Yet, as the Thatcher government withdraws state-funding to the arts, sports and charity, the void has to be filled. Business must play its part if the quality of life of the country is not to sink to unacceptable levels.

If this altruistic argument does not convince, there is a more compelling commercial argument. Business needs a stable, well-ordered society in which to prosper. A society constantly in ferment, because of racial tensions such as we saw with the riots in Brixton, Bristol, Birmingham, Southall and latterly Bradford, is not a society which is favourable to business efficiency. It is significant that although the Marks & Spencer store at Brixton was right in the middle of the rioting, it was neither attacked nor looted. Perhaps it had something to do with the fact that the directors had over many years developed a policy of community and charitable activity.

For me there were other emotions at play. The employees of NFC had done very well out of their investment. The success had come from making better use of what once were state-owned assets. We had more reasons than most for wanting to give something back to society.

At the AGM in 1985, in a document called 'The Way Ahead', we proposed a series of measures that, when implemented, would put us up with the leading companies in the UK in our social and community responsibility programmes. We started as usual from the premise that any money to be spent on these programmes had to have the shareholders' approval. After all, it is *their* money and while I would not want to reduce in any way the support that business gives to charity and community care, I do believe that the directors of all public companies should first have a mandate from the shareholders for their programmes. If such a mandate was sought at each AGM, the result might surprise many, as I believe shareholders as a whole would tend to be more generous than is currently the case when the decision is taken solely by the board.

We attacked this issue in our usual consultative way. We needed the programmes to be funded. To do this we put two resolutions to shareholders. First, that 1 per cent of the share capital of the company should be given to a trust whose major role would be to alleviate hardship among employees and pensioners. At the time of the gift the value of the NFC was less than £100m. Consequently, it was a modest trust we established. It nevertheless had the unanimous approval of the shareholders. Today the trust has a value of nearly £9m and the dividends it receives are now worth over £300,000 per annum. A great deal of hardship can be alleviated with this income. The second resolution proposed that the directors could progressively allocate up to ½ per cent of pre-tax profits to charity and community work. Once ½ per cent was reached in 1988, there was a further resolution at the 1989 AGM continuing the upward allocation until 1 per cent of pre-tax profits will be reached by 1990. So we now had the financial base to be a useful player in the growing band of businesses who are involved in community work. We more than qualify for The Percent Club, so well promoted by Sir Hector Laing, the chairman of United Biscuits. This club is made up of companies who give more than ½ per cent of their pre-tax profits to charity.

Having allocated the money, we then asked our shareholders how they wanted it to be spent. Their views were sought by yet another MORI survey of shareholders' views. The survey revealed some strongly-held views. As a first priority the shareholders wanted the company to look after the wellbeing of our own pensioners. They demanded a higher level of care than we had provided in the past. They were more than happy to give money to medical, children's and old people's charities, but *not* to arts, education, sport and culture. They would have no part in donations to political parties. (This surprised me a little. After all, it was a political act by the Conservative Party that was the basis of the wealth they were enjoying.)

Whether we agreed with it or not, we now knew exactly what they wanted us to do with the available money. We felt, and they agreed, that the best way of ensuring that the charity funds were well and caringly administered was to put them in the hands of a partially elected body to be named the Social Responsibilities Council. An AGM resolution was passed setting this up. The council started work under the chairmanship of Frank Law, who had now retired from the main board. He willingly took up the new task, as it is a world that is near and dear to his heart. A wide range of initiatives has emerged in a relatively short period of time.

The first thing to be tackled was the 23,000 pensioners. In the days of state ownership, we paid them a pension and we did nothing more. We set forth to rectify this. We asked the more active pensioners to work with us to establish a visiting scheme. We knew that many of our frail and elderly pensioners were lonely and had problems. The hope was that they could be visited regularly by another pensioner. If there were problems, the visitor could help to sort them out, and if the solution required finance, there was money available from the trust.

The next step was to encourage pensioners to form themselves into groups in every part of the country. The purposes were social. They could organize lunches, lectures, dances and day trips. In less than four years there are now 48 active pensioner groups. Keeping links with old colleagues is a deep-rooted need in many that NFC had done little to recognize. One of the best-read publications is the bi-monthly magazine sent to all pensioners called, appropriately, *Changing Gear*! Good businesses have been doing these sorts of things for years. As a nationalized industry, which in concept was supposed to have a caring face, it didn't happen. It is yet another example of how a political solution does not necessarily create the right culture in which the needs of the individual are paramount.

In addition to pensioner care, the Social Responsibilities Council has supported many charities, particularly topping up the fund-raising activities of our own employees in their own communities. The causes they have supported have been wide-ranging; from giving to the Lockerbie air crash disaster, because we had an old-established depot in the town, to support for the starving in East Africa – including sending out one of our managers to help with the transport problems of delivering the relief food to the remote regions of the Sudan.

Latterly the Council has developed programmes for giving help in the community to the underprivileged and handicapped. We have concentrated on helping them to start their own businesses, or to acquire skills to make them more independent and to reduce their need for social security help.

It is hard to find a causal relationship, but it cannot be coincidence that the majority of the really successful companies see the need to play a full role in community support projects. I guess it is one of the values in a business that makes the better people want to work for it. As I have repeatedly said, in a service industry it is the quality of the workforce that gives the marketing edge. We must therefore have values which appeal to the best.

We do not want NFC's employee ownership to be measured solely by profitability, the value of the shares and the number of millionaires it has created, but by whether a company is emerging that has a culture and values that are respected by its own employees and in the wider community in which it does its business. That is a higher hurdle to jump, but we believe we are on the way.

8

Flotation

'This little piggy went to market' . . .

From the first day of the buy-out there were three potential spectres at the feast. The first was the fear that if it were a great success, it would only be those who had had the foresight, courage or wherewithal to buy shares at the beginning who would benefit. Instead of the 'us and them' of workers and management, a different 'us and them' would appear – those whose capital stake was growing exponentially and those who had no stake at all.

Secondly, we recognized that the internal market where we buy and sell shares would one day run out of buying power. This had never happened, but there was the mathematical certainty that one day it would happen. In 1981, after a prolonged and intensive communications exercise, we only managed to raise £7m from our employee family. In 1987 some £18.3m of shares changed hands on the internal stock market. If the day came when family members wanted to sell a share and there was no buyer, the currency would be debased. The shareholders could take the view that theirs were not 'real' shares and there was no 'real' value in them.

The third spectre was the most depressing of all. It was almost inevitable, because of the potential lack of buying power in our own market, that we would have to seek a stock market listing. At this time the shares would have a full value. This in turn could result in a stampede to sell, and thus within a decade from start to finish NFC would become like any other company with the vast majority of its shares owned by the City institutions. It would then have been a short-term phenomenon; interesting, but having no long-term significance; an unstable concept from the beginning – a shooting star that rose to the heavens and burnt out in a split second of history. We felt the concept was worth more than this. So we set to work to remove all three spectres from the feast!

We started work on these problems as early as in 1984. We first addressed them in a document I have already mentioned called 'The Way Ahead' which was put to the shareholders for their approval at the AGM in 1986. The first problem it dealt with was how to tackle the 'fat cat' syndrome, as I called it. There we were, the 'fat cats', who had been around in 1982. Our investments had by 1989 multiplied in value a hundred times. Why should the succeeding generations work enthusiastically to make the 'fat cats' even fatter if there was nothing in it for them? We had to ensure that there was something in it for everybody.

The concept we put forward was that each year we should allocate 25 per cent of pre-tax profits for profit-sharing in shares, to be given to the employees who had created that year's profits. While our non-employee shareholders were liberal and in tune with our beliefs of the value of employee motivation, they did feel that 25 per cent was a bit much. The guideline for profit-sharing by the City investor protection societies is no more than 5 per cent of UK profit before tax. After a little negotiation, principally with the leader of the banking syndicate which held 17½ per cent of the equity, we dropped the level of allocation to 15 per cent. This would only be payable in full if pretty stiff targets of growth in earnings per share were met.

We then had to make the 15 per cent punch more than its weight in recycling employee share ownership. Philip Mayo dreamt up a unique scheme which he managed to sell to the Inland Revenue, thus making it tax effective. It was, for tax purposes, one scheme, but it had two parts. Part A was designed to encourage employees to save for shares. Each employee could save annually up to 3 per cent of his salary. If he kept up the monthly payments for twelve months, the share trust would buy the shares he had saved for. They would then add a bonus of one extra share for every three the employee had bought with his

164

savings. The scheme was designed to encourage people through saving to own more shares.

The more capital stake an individual has in the company, the more committed to its success he is likely to be. The clever operator, unless we prevented him, could sell some of his existing shares and use the money to invest in the savings scheme. He would thus be receiving one-third more shares than he had sold, and at the end of the year he would not be any more committed to the company through his share ownership. So we ruled out 'round tripping', as we called it. To qualify for the bonus shares an individual had to finish the year with more shares in owner-ship than the number with which he started the year.

The second part of the scheme was a straight giveaway of shares to everyone in the company who had worked for the full year in which the profits had been made. Some of the fiercest debate we had at the meetings held throughout the country to explain the scheme was how to allocate the bonus shares. The formula proposed by the board was a few shares for length of service plus a minimum base number of shares, with the vast majority of the shares being allocated according to the salary earned – a given number of shares for each £1000 of salary. We argued that salary was the only way we had of measuring the contribution to the overall profit of each individual. Many of the less well-paid were incensed and felt the concept was divisive – everyone should receive the same. At the other end of the scale a number of senior management felt it should be tilted more in favour of the top management who took the major decisions by which most of the company's success was won. The majority of British industry rewarded this (our top management claimed) by making share options available in large quantity to the select few at the top. After much debate at the regional meetings, and finally at the AGM, the original scheme went ahead with the minor modification of giving a little more for length of service. But it has left us with a future problem of how to ensure we have an employment package to attract whatever top senior management we need to recruit from outside.

The vital issue was what effect this scheme would have on young men entering NFC service today. Can we ever make their capital stake significant? To help me answer this I enlisted the aid of one of those young men, Philip Roe, a 22-year-old economics graduate, who had worked for us for only a year. He realized that the variables were so many that the only way to tackle the problem was to create a computer model.

Among the variables were: NFC's share price and financial performance, salary progression of individuals, retirement of existing shareholders, rate of sale of shares by existing share-holders, the per cent of pre-tax profits given to profit-sharing, the percentage of employees who take shares and the percentage that takes the cash alternative, and so forth. It was hardly surprising that my back-of-the-envelope calculations to see whether it was possible on the one hand to make capitalists of a new generation of workers and on the other to retain employee control of the company were pretty pathetic when contrasted with the power of Philip Roe's computer model.

What the model showed was that if NFC could increase its earnings per share by 15 per cent per annum average for the next eleven years (for the first six it has averaged over 30 per cent growth per annum but we did recognize that the hill was getting steeper), and if employees took full part in both profit-sharing schemes, and assuming the Stock Exchange gave NFC an average PE rating of 14 (in fact this rating stands today at around 18), we could create a new generation of employee capitalists.

The driver joining today would have a stake in the NFC worth £50,000 by the year 2000 – almost twice the level of what he would be earning then. The graduate joining today, assuming he has six promotions in twelve years, would have a stake of around £86,000. If we were to recruit a new board member, his stake on the assumptions made would be worth £400,000. From this we concluded that it was possible to prevent the 'fat cat' syndrome biting too deeply into our corporate culture. With the right level of communication we should be able to motivate new employees with the possibility of receiving a large and worthwhile capital stake.

The second spectre at the feast was that the internal market would run out of buying power. I became excessively concerned about this – in the event, because we recognized the possibility and took steps to prevent it happening, it never did. I was worried that a 'run on the bank' might happen. Everyone is happy

166

enough to leave their money in the bank as long as they believe that if they ever want it, they can withdraw it. Although it doesn't figure strongly in their thought processes, depositors know that if everyone at the same time demanded their money back, the bank could not meet these demands. If a rumour starts that a bank is in difficulty, the immediate reaction of everyone is to behave like Gadarene swine. They all rush to draw out their money and thus ensure that the bank will go under and that they will never all get their money back.

NFC's problems were not as dramatic as this, but I had a similar scenario at the back of my mind. We had the limited group of people to whom we could sell our shares – the employees and their families. The total demand for shares was therefore limited to the buying power which could be generated by the family. There was a chance that if NFC's results went off, the demand for shares could dry up. At the same time, the wish of the family to sell would be increased because many more people would be wanting to realize some or all of their investment. As with a normal market, the price of the shares could not plummet until it found a new, lower equilibrium, as it was not part of the valuer's brief to try to balance precisely buyers and sellers. It was not part of his valuation process to clear the market. The result would be that we would have many unwilling holders of shares who would feel locked in. They would begin to question the validity of the share certificate. After all, if you can't sell a share when you want to, you must begin to feel that the certificate you hold is pretty worthless. The disillusionment would be total.

First of all we put in place a kind of safety net made up of institutional investors. Fortunately the value of the holding of NFC unquoted shares owned by the original syndicate of banks was becoming too heavy for the venture and development capital companies of some of the banks. They wanted to sell a portion of their holdings. They were happy for us to make presentations to about twenty of the larger investment institutions inviting them to buy some of the surplus bank shares. If they bought, the understanding was that if on any of the dealing days there was a surplus of sellers over buyers, the new institutional investors would be prepared to come in and clear the market by buying the surplus shares. By agreeing to provide this safety net, they needed to satisfy themselves that the valuer was not an optimist. Quite the opposite. The way he valued the shares was conservative! Fifteen of the institutions took part in the umbrella.

By accepting these institutions as shareholders, we had taken on board another pressure group who would want to see NFC as a fully-listed company on the London Stock Exchange at some time. This safety net fulfilled the role of all good safety nets – it was never actually needed. But it gave the confidence to the existing investors to keep on buying – and this demand, coupled with continued good trading performance, meant a constantly rising dealing price (except for the dealing day after Black Monday).

However, the reality of arithmetic could not be bucked for ever. The value of the company was going up each year. When we started, the NFC was valued at £7.5m. By 1987 it had reached £419m on the internal market. When we finally came to be listed on the London Stock Exchange in 1989, it had a market capitalization of nearly £900 million. We observed that approximately 5 per cent of the shares changed hands each year. So in the first year the buying power needed by the family to satisfy all the sellers was less than £1m. By 1989 the buying power required would have been £45m, and I estimate £200m by the end of the century. It was unrealistic to believe that the employees could find these sums of money. We concluded that the NFC would inevitably have to come to the Stock Exchange at some stage. The questions were when and how.

The timing was reasonably easy to decide. We obviously needed to find a time before the internal buying power ran out and when the stock market was in a generally bullish state. With the collapse of the market following Black Monday in 1987, we clearly had to allow the bear market to abate. We judged that at the earliest this would be at the end of 1988 or early 1989.

Exactly how we approached the Stock Exchange required much more consideration. As part of our business mission we were committed 'to retain employee control'. Our common sense told us that without some mechanism to make employee shares more significant in voting power than other shares, it would be impossible to maintain employee control over the vital decisions made in the business. In particular we wanted control over the most vital decision of all – who would actually own and run the company if it was ever subjected to a takeover bid. These issues were being debated at a time when the business world was concerned about the plethora of takeovers that were happening in the USA and UK. Workforces were being traded almost daily as takeovers were finalized between owners without any consideration of employees' views or wishes.

I was in the office of an American whose company had been taken over three times in four years. While I was there, his new boss rang him. Such was the cynicism his reply to his secretary was, 'Take his name, I'll ring him back.' In 1987 the takeover issue dominated the CBI conference to such an extent that the President, to appease the warring factions – the industrialists and the City – went through the time-honoured heat-evaporation ritual of setting up a joint City/industry working party. It concluded some fifteen months later that there really wasn't a problem, or that if there was, it only needed the whitewash brush of better communication to be applied. However, this does not remove the fact that the issue of takeovers was (and still is) the fear of many industrialists and many of their workforces. It was certainly exercising the minds of the NFC board at the time.

We also recognized that the retirement of many of the bigger shareholders was forthcoming. The executives with sizeable holdings were setting up family trusts to protect their holding against the ravages of taxation, and these shares, once in trust, were no longer technically employee-owned shares. In addition, many large shareholders were being told by their financial advisers that it was unwise to have all their capital eggs in one business basket. Finally, some shareholders were naturally expecting to see some of their paper wealth being transferred into real wealth. They wanted to buy the good things in life – extra holidays, second homes, better cars and better household furnishings. All this meant that there would be an inevitable erosion of employee share ownership. The major counterattack to this erosion was the profit-sharing scheme which would buy existing family shares and recycle them to the next generation of employees. We also had an expanding workforce whom we would continue to encourage to buy shares as soon as they became part of NFC.

Despite this recycling process, we still needed extra voting power to be given to the employees if they were to be the prime decision-takers on the future ownership of NFC well into the twenty-first century. We decided that we would endow the employee shares with double voting rights. The double vote would apply on one issue and one issue only – the prospective takeover of the company. We were not seeking any feather-bedding for the directors. If they were incompetent they could and should be got rid of, as any board of directors of any company, by a majority vote of the shareholders. But we were determined that if a predator sought to take over NFC, the deal could not be fixed without the predator winning the votes of the employees. With their double voting right no predator could succeed without at least having the employees substantially on his side. We were not going to be a party to the selling of NFC over the heads of its employees. Apart from this there was another principle at play. A man who commits both his money and his working life to a company should surely have more say about its future than someone who has merely invested his money.

The mechanism required to achieve this, and for which we sought the shareholders' agreement, was unusual. It concentrated solely on the takeover procedure. Under the proposed new NFC articles, no one was allowed to hold more than 8 per cent of NFC's shares. If they went beyond 8 per cent, the directors could require the individual to sell all the excess shares, which would in any case be disenfranchised – they would not have voting rights. If he refused to divest, the board had the power to sell the shares on his behalf. This meant that at a relatively early stage in any takeover battle, the predator had to come out into the open. If he wanted to proceed with the takeover, he had to call a general meeting to seek to have amended the particular clauses in the Articles of Association which prevented him from buying more shares. This would be the central issue on which a debate could take place, and on which a vote would have to be taken. It would be on this issue that the double voting right of the employees came into play.

Most takeovers do not have a central debate. Voters use their own judgement and the takeover process trickles to a con-clusion. This was not the way NFC had taken its important decisions in the past, and it was not the way we wished to take the most important decision of all – who would own the company in the future.

Before putting these new articles in place in 1986, we did seek out the views of future investors. Helped by Kitcat & Aitken, the stockbrokers who had shown interest in NFC from the beginning, we gathered together a group of the top pension and insurance fund managers. We presented them with the dilemma as we saw it.

Our phenomenal success had in part come from employee ownership. When we came to the market, investors would buy the shares because of that track record. If obtaining a Stock Exchange listing meant that the control of the company passed into the hands of the City, we would become no different from other companies and the marketing edge of employee control would disappear. Therefore, if not handled carefully, flotation could kill the goose that was laying the golden eggs. In these circumstances we asked the potential investors to accept NFC as a special case and agree to differential voting rights. At both lunches the debate was fierce. At one end of the scale there were the doyens of the two investor protection groups who were totally against any form of differential voting rights: one share – one vote and no deviation. At the other end were many who recognized the problem and said that the double voting right would only mean a marginally lower price as the potential takeover premium would go out of the shares. It was a helpful discussion but at the end of it we knew we would have to make our own decisions.

Accordingly the AGM in 1986 adopted a new set of articles which incorporated the double vote. It was to prove to be a difficult issue for the Stock Exchange when we applied for a listing some four years later.

With the safety net in place we had a temporary respite that enabled us to take our time over the next step.

We were also coming under pressure to go public. Questions were being asked both at the shareholders' meetings and also at the AGM. One pensioner, Jack Butler, stood up in 1987 and compared the internal dealing price unfavourably with the price of the shares of our competitors who were listed on the Stock

Exchange. He asked why the board was not recommending flotation – what were we afraid of?

What I was afraid of, deep down, was that unless we judged the flotation exactly right and gave to the family shareholders exactly the right leadership message, the arrival of NFC on the stock market would lead to a rush of selling. The employee share-ownership values of NFC would disappear as the majority of the shares found their way into the hands of City institutions. But we couldn't isolate ourselves from the mounting pressure to float. We had committed ourselves in the original prospectus issued at the time of the buy-out not to seek a Stock Exchange quotation for at least five years, but after that time we had undertaken to raise the issue at every AGM. This commitment made certain the matter would not go away. Each year we would have to justify why we were still taking the view not to float the company.

Perhaps the most persistent pressure came because I knew that the majority of the senior management wanted to see their shares have the strength of a market quote. They had considerable stakes in the company. Unquoted shares do not carry the same weight as quoted shares if used as collateral. For example, they will not be taken into account by Lloyds where in order to be a 'name' in an underwriting syndicate you have to demonstrate that you have assets of at least £250,000. Similarly, bank managers will not normally accept unquoted shares as collateral against a loan, although in the latter stages we were able to agree with one or two of the major banks that they would lend up to 60 per cent of the dealing day value even though the shares were unquoted. In addition, members of this key group more than any other group of shareholders understood that there was an inherent discount to a fair market price in the internal market. I could not risk their disillusionment – NFC needed their total commitment if it was to continue with its aggressive expansion.

The pressures were growing – five years was up! Yet again it was time to set up a working group to weigh up the pros and cons of going to the market. I chaired this group. Its deliberations were dominated by constant debate about the values of the NFC. There could be no long-term argument against the arithmetic. What convinced me finally that it was time to go was the realization that by going to market the responsibility for the future of employee ownership would be transferred to the only place it should ever rest – with the individual shareholder. His decision would be untrammelled by any protective walls that had circled the company to date. He would decide whether he valued employee ownership. If *he* didn't, why should the board continue to strive for something which he did not value?

So the decision on the future of employee ownership would rest with the employees. They would each make up their own minds about whether to hold on to their shares, buy more, or sell. The collective effect of all these individual decisions was the only judgement that was worth anything, if you believe, as I do, in the basic common sense of the individual. It was their company; they had had some seven years to taste and savour the new values. It was up to them to decide whether they wanted these values to survive. 'By their actions shall you know them.' Their individual actions would decide the collective future. The working group therefore recommended flotation and this was accepted by the board.

Before we put the recommendation to the shareholders, we knew we had to give more shape to the recommendation. We had to decide how the company would come to the market. This involved more months of debate. It was the central theme of the 1987 Chairman's conference which was attended by the top one hundred managers – the same group that in 1981 gave overwhelming support to the original buy-out. From these debates we edged towards the basis on which we could recommend flotation. The issues were simple but often conflicting. On the one hand we had to do nothing which would mean that on flotation employee ownership would fly out of the window. This meant that we had to put a ceiling on the amount of new money we would raise. On the other hand, we still had much debt on and off balance sheet which we had to try to reduce. Flotation gave us the opportunity to do this. The market values companies with little debt more highly than companies that are debt-laden when there is a prospect of a downturn in the economy. Debt-free companies tend to weather economic downturns better than companies who have high interest costs to pay. But every new

173

share we issued to raise new money meant that share potentially going out of family hands. It was unlikely that the existing shareholders would have the available money to buy the new shares we would be issuing.

The matter was fiercely contested. The accountants wanted to use flotation to clear up the balance sheet. They argued we should raise over £150m in new money. Others, myself included, put more value on employee control. We argued that we had in the past managed well and pushed aggressively earnings per share by using debt. Why not continue the same formula in the future? As usual a compromise was reached and the recommendation emerged that not more than £100m new money should be raised. By this decision, we effectively put a ceiling of 15 per cent on the possible level of family dilution as a result of raising new money at flotation.

The next matter was the double voting provisions. It was argued by some that the City in general, and the Stock Exchange in particular, would not like this. They could well refuse the NFC a listing because of it. At the very least it would mean that the shares would get a lower market rating. We should therefore discard it. Many more were captured by the argument that we had to preserve employee control even if it might mean a lower market price. This view finally won the day. The AGM resolution was that there would be no change in the NFC Articles which contained the double vote for employees on a threatened takeover. We recognized that a commitment now to the way in which we would exercise the double vote might prove an obstacle when we started the negotiations with the Stock Exchange, so we did not tie ourselves to an exact procedure. But the resolution, because no change in the Articles was specifically proposed, meant we had to get agreement for the double voting rights from the Stock Exchange or we could not bring the company to market.

The exact wording of the key resolution agreed by the Chairman's conference was as follows:

> The board be authorized to seek a listing of the issued ordinary shares of 5p each in the capital of the company on the Stock Exchange London by means of an introduc-

tion at the most appropriate time within the next two years. At its discretion it may also raise up to £100m new money by way of a Rights Issue.

To explain what all this meant, again, we held many meetings around the country. The shareholders had to know exactly what flotation implied and the mechanism by which we intended to get there. Everyone received an array of pamphlets and broadsheets seeking to answer the many questions and to allay the concerns that many smaller shareholders had about the stock market. We invited them all to the AGM in Blackpool to take the decision collectively.

More than four thousand people turned up on that wet, cold Sunday morning in February. The debate was not long but all the issues were raised. I opened by saying we could not wallow in nostalgia. Many would argue it had all been so good. So why change? But we had to look forward. The future depended upon the personal decision of each of them, on whether, individually, they valued the concept of employee ownership.

All the other major issues were raised. The first three or four speakers concentrated on the possibility of takeover and asset stripping if we were on the market. The pro-marketeers fought back by asking what we were afraid of. If we were successful we could be the predators. In any case only unsuccessful companies were taken over. It was more than time we had a fair price for the shares. Others worried about how they would trade shares in the future. They had become used to our customer-friendly dealing system. Stockbrokers were alien creatures, as were their complex share-buying and selling methods.

After about an hour's debate I put the resolution to the meeting. It was carried overwhelmingly. Now our task was to find the right way to bring the employee-owned NFC to market without damaging its values in the process. We had two years to do it – if we could not find the right market environment or acceptance of the double voting rights, we would have to seek a new mandate.

It became obvious, early on, that the best time for us to seek a listing was either in late 1988 or early 1989. As we will see, there are many rules governing the listing of a company. One of the more straightforward rules is that the company has to come to the market with audited results which are less than six months old. Our year end was 1 October. The 1988 results were looking good. We would normally have our audited results available by December, so we could go to the market on the 1988 results at any time between December and March. This seemed a good time to target. The exact date is really in the lap of the gods. Until almost the last day, no one can be sure that the market sentiment will be right. For example, a good number of new issues were pulled during the weeks after the collapse of the world stock market following Black Monday in 1987. We planned for early 1989, but we recognized that market conditions would always ultimately decide.

9

City Innocents

'If the goose lays golden eggs, are you going
to shoot it?'
Financial Times, 15 February 1986

It was now April 1988 and time to move into flotation mode.
This signalled involvement with most of the major factions that
collectively are called 'the City'. Most businessmen do not ever
have the doubtful pleasure of taking one company to market. I
must have sinned against the deity who presides over business
as, in the space of two months, it was my misfortune to take two
companies to market. I say 'misfortune' because, while the
process is exciting and generates much adrenalin, it is expensive
and consumes senior management time, and most of the effort
is neither creative nor does it improve the quality of the business
which is being taken to market.

The process that led to both NFC and a much smaller health-
care company called Community Hospitals coming to the market
almost at the same time started within a month of each other in
the spring of 1981. It was then that the early moves were made
that led to the buy-out of NFC from government. At about the
same time I had a phone call, out of the blue, from Robin
Hodgson. I did not know, but soon found out, that he was the
managing director of a small City finance house which was at
the time called Nightingales, and today is known as Granvilles.
Nightingales was a business that was going through difficult
times and had made a heavy loss the previous year. Robin
Hodgson was slowly turning the company around. He was an
unusual man with great business talents coupled with deep

political convictions. He had been an MP and had won the Walsall seat for the Conservatives in a by-election in 1976. John Stonehouse, the Labour minister, had to vacate the seat following his much-publicized disappearing act. (Having left his clothes on a beach in Rio to give the impression that he had drowned, he later turned up in Australia and was jailed for a variety of financial offences.) At the next election the seat returned to Labour, so Robin Hodgson returned to the business world and took over as MD of Nightingales. In the meantime, private health in the UK received an unexpected fillip from Barbara Castle. As Minister of Health in the Callaghan government, she decided to phase out private beds from the National Health Service. Perversely this proved to be the incentive for the growth of the commercial private health-care sector in Britain. Robin Hodgson recognized the opportunity and decided to set up an investment company to channel funds into the building of private hospitals. Many local doctor/consultant initiatives were now emerging. Denied access to the NHS, many consultants were seeking alternative ways of continuing their private practices.

Robin Hodgson realized that if the new investment company was to have credibility and attract City funds, it had to have a strong board of directors with a businessman as chairman. Through his political contacts he managed to get a short list of businessmen who had had any connection with health. My name was on it because for a number of years I had been the British Institute of Management's nominee on the board of governors of one of the London teaching hospitals – The Royal National Throat, Nose & Ear Hospital in Gray's Inn Road. I had witnessed at first hand how the consensus management style of the NHS frustrated any attempt to improve the efficiency of the hospital services. It made me quite certain that it was not a style of management to adopt if the efficient use of scarce resources was in part the purpose of the enterprise. It took the report by Sir Roy Griffiths of Sainsbury's some seven years later to point out the need for accountable management if the NHS was to be made more efficient and give better-value health care.

After two or three discussions Robin Hodgson invited me to chair the new company. So the long road that finally resulted in NFC and Community Hospitals being brought to market started at almost the same time. It is a complete coincidence that they arrived at the door of the Stock Exchange seeking admission at the same time.

Therefore, almost uniquely, I watched over the process of flotation of two very different companies. From this experience I have severe reservations about the process. I am certain that if London wants to keep its place as a major financial centre, it needs to re-examine the cost and procedures that new companies seeking a listing on the Stock Exchange have to suffer. There must be a simpler way of achieving what is after all a simple objective: that of inviting new investors to buy shares in a company that has to have a five-year audited track record to be considered for flotation on the main Stock Exchange.

The City puts great demand upon the company wishing to be quoted on the Stock Exchange. These demands are not from the Stock Exchange alone, although their requirements cause most of the work load; but also from the many players and advisers who are involved in the course of the company seeking admission to the Stock Exchange. The system demands that advice must be taken. The need for the advice is sometimes obvious and sensible, but frequently the need is less apparent. One has to suspect that vested interest comes into play. The more the advice – the greater the fees. In deciding whether my criticism is fair, it has to be remembered that the City advisers go through these processes all the time; the company seeking admission but once. The board of the company therefore tend to take the advice they are given, just as an individual doing a parachute jump but once for charity tends not to challenge the advice of the instructor.

The first piece of advice given is that you must assemble a team of advisers to help you. I will list the team. It is difficult to imagine that anything or anyone could need so much advice and protection just in order to invite some new investors to buy some shares in the company.

You need a sponsor, usually a merchant bank. This is a Stock Exchange requirement. I assume this is because they do not want to deal face to face with every new company that seeks to have its stock quoted on their market. Such an attitude is alien to most businessmen. After all, shares in companies are only the products that the stock market, through its members, sells and buys for its customers, the general public or the institutions. The stock market is in reality only a trading entity like a retail chain. No retailer, such as Sainsbury's or Marks & Spencer, would say to its suppliers, 'Do not deal with us direct, you must go through our nominated agent before we will stock your product.' The process of vetting a company's worthiness to have its shares quoted is akin to the quality control procedure that a retailer insists on before he will sell a manufacturer's product. I cannot imagine a retailer ever wanting to delegate this responsibility to a third party. But the Stock Exchange, for reasons best known to itself, does not want to do its own quality-controlling, so you have to have a sponsor – in our case Barclays Merchant Bank. It isn't even that the rush of companies is too great for the Stock Exchange to handle. NFC and Community Hospitals were the only new entrants to the market in the first five months of 1989.

James Watson, the deputy chairman, and I had many invitations to lunch from merchant banks in the months leading up to flotation. Taking a company to market is a lucrative activity for the sponsor, and hence the competition to be appointed is fierce. In our case, although we enjoyed the lunches, there was never really any doubt that Barclays would be our sponsor. Without their vision in 1981, NFC as an employee-owned business would not have got off the ground. Debts of this magnitude demand loyalty and we were happy, if we had to have a sponsor, for it to be Barclays.

The sponsor's first advice was to tell us what additional advisers we would need. For now it is not just NFC's reputation that is at stake, but also the reputation of the sponsor. Inevitably we must have lawyers. Not just one set, but at least two. At one stage during flotation we had no less than eleven firms of lawyers working for the sponsors or ourselves on one matter or another. The minimum, however, is two sets of lawyers – one to look after the company's interests, the other to look after the sponsor's. I soon found it pointless arguing that the interests of the company and the sponsors were surely the same. We both want to present a fair prospectus to the new investors on which they should buy the shares. The hallowed process of flotation does not accept this.

The principal role of both sets of lawyers is to make sure that the company does not make any statement in the prospectus or elsewhere that could be held to be misleading to the potential

180

investor. The centrepiece of this process is verification. Every word and phrase is dissected and the author is required to prove it to be true. It took many man-weeks of lawyer and company management time to go through this process. I am not sure much of significance was taken out of the original draft of the prospectus, but what is certain is that any phrase indicating feeling, instinct or emotion was watered down by the process of verification to rice-pudding banality. The lawyers claim this process works, as few company directors have been prosecuted for issuing a false prospectus. Nor have many directors been taken to court by investors because they bought shares as a result of a misleading prospectus.

At some point when I was feeling particularly frustrated by the process, I asked our sponsor when the last time was that anyone had committed the dire crime from which we were being saved at vast expense. He said it was a road haulier in the mid-1950s. This, the sponsor argued, showed what a good job the legal profession was doing. I think it is more akin to the man tearing up newspapers into small pieces and throwing them out of the train window on to the railway line. When asked why he was doing it he said, 'It helps to keep the wild elephants away.'

'But there are no wild elephants in the UK.'

'I know, so you can see how effective it is.'

I do doubt whether there are many, if any, directors of public companies coming to the market who want the share price to be artificially boosted by making false or inaccurate statements. Through time the verification process has become longer and longer as lawyers working continuously on prospectuses find ever-more clever legal points that have to be covered. Enough is enough. Someone needs to blow the whistle and stop this legal merry-go-round.

The next thing the sponsor required of us was reporting accountants. 'Ah,' we sighed with relief, 'we already have those.' Our accountants are the respected international firm of Ernst & Whinney. Each year they audit our accounts and certify them as being true and fair. No problem here, we thought; all we have to do is string together the five-year record from the published audited accounts and that will surely satisfy the most fastidious of potential investors. 'Not enough,' cried the sponsor in need of even more protection from the potentially aggrieved investor. Or perhaps the motive is to be certain that he is doing a thorough job of quality control on behalf of the Stock Exchange. The sponsor demanded a long form report. This entailed the same firm of auditors revisiting every one of our 70 subsidiaries and re-examining and re-presenting the accounts which they had already certified were a true and fair record. It meant many months of work not only for the team of professional accountants from Ernst & Whinney but also for the managements within the NFC subsidiaries who had to do most of the work.

At the end we were presented with two things. First, a bookcase full of 'long form' reports which confirmed the bookcase full of certified annual accounts which we already had. Secondly, Ernst & Whinney submitted their bill for over £1m. I do not believe that a 'long form' report is necessary when a company has a history of audited accounts. I am sure that if potential investors were asked whether they want protection or whether they would prefer an extra £1m to strengthen the cash flow of the company, they would choose the money.

Next we needed a stockbroker. The principal role of the stockbroker is to sell the shares to the investors. The company seeking a listing is the client of the stockbroker. But his *regular* clients are the pension and investment fund managers for whom they daily buy and sell large quantities of shares. Since Big Bang, the larger brokers also 'make the market' in the shares: that is, they fix the price which seeks to match buyers and sellers. They take the risk of holding stocks of shares. They will even buy and sell shares when they have no stock. They take the risk that they will be able to buy or sell at a later date. Market-making is a high-risk game and since Big Bang many have lost money at it. Stockbroking involves less risk. The larger stockbrokers also now offer their clients corporate financial advice. As a consequence the role of the sponsor and the stockbroker is becoming blurred. Barclays de Zoete Wedd, for example, could have been the sponsors and also, through their stockbroking subsidiary, the brokers. Similarly, Phillips & Drew the stockbrokers could have been the sponsors. In fact, as the NFC float progressed, Phillips & Drew became not only our main stockbroker but also the joint sponsor. The vertical integration of financial services has escalated leading up to and following Big Bang, and consequently the role of the players is becoming more confused.

The company coming to the market must realize that the stockbroker is on his side until it comes to fixing the price at which the shares are offered to the public. At this stage there is a conflict of interest. On the one hand, the company coming to the market is his client and he wants to do the best for him. On the other hand, the frequent buyers and sellers of shares – the institutions – are all his *regular* clients and he wants them to have a good deal out of the issue. In other words, he wants the price to be low enough so that they make a profit when dealing starts. So when it comes to pricing an issue the company coming to the market cannot rely totally on the advice of the broker.

It is here that the sponsor should be more helpful. His role in part is to ensure that the price of the offer is fair. But again, unfortunately, in a normal Stock Exchange listing he also has a conflict of interest. The sponsor normally arranges the underwriting of the shares. Underwriting is the process by which the company wishing to raise money when coming to the market is guaranteed that it will actually get the money it needs. For a cost of about 2 per cent (on big issues it will be lower), the sponsor provides what is in effect the insurance against any stock on offer being left over. This guarantees that at the asking price all the shares will be bought. If the market will not buy them, the underwriter buys them.

Underwriting the issue is usually a lucrative operation because only rarely does an issue fail. The price is usually fixed at a level so that all the shares are bought; and as a result the underwriting commission is all profit. Like all good gamblers, the sponsor lays off some of the risk with sub-underwriters. The sub-underwriters are usually the same institutions who will be buying the shares. The carrot of involvement in the sub-underwriting provides an additional incentive to ensure that the investment or pension fund buys its quota of shares. Sub-underwriting commission is thus an extra safeguard against the issue being a failure. But it all costs money to the shareholders of the company coming to the market. Due to his role as an underwriter, the sponsor has an incentive to fix the price of the shares on the low side.

These conflicts of interest do raise doubts as to whether the owners of the company being floated are truly getting the best price available in the market conditions. The reality is that the existing owners of the company have to fight their own corner on price – nobody else is in there with them. Indeed, there are so many conflicts of interest that the system depends upon the integrity of individuals.

A better system perhaps would start with the not unreasonable assumption that the directors of the company coming to the market have integrity themselves. The present system assumes that most companies will want to present an over-optimistic view of their companies in order to sell the shares. Additionally, the buyers of shares are likely to be litigious if for any reason they lose money as a result of a new share issue. The directors must be prevented from doing the former and protected against the latter by an army of expensive advisers. Before suggesting a possible solution I must introduce the last set of advisers – the City public relations men.

Their role in life is to see that the company presents itself in as advantageous a way as possible to the media and to potential investors. It is always difficult to assess their contribution. All you can be sure of is that it will be expensive. They will want to make certain that your promotional kit is in pristine condition. You will need a new corporate brochure, probably a new corporate video and certainly the amateurish way that you have for years presented your annual reports will no longer do. After all, you will now be addressing a more sophisticated set of investors if you are to be listed on the International Stock Exchange of London.

If the listing is to be by way of an offer for sale, the law will require you to print in full the whole prospectus in at least two national papers. It beggars logic why on earth, like any other product being offered for sale, the interested buyer cannot be invited in a concise advert to apply for the prospectus. Four or five full pages in the *Financial Times* does not come cheap. I wonder how many potential investors plough through the whole prospectus in a daily newspaper? If he is interested, surely he would prefer to read the published prospectus. All this means that the PR and advertising bill will be high, and will probably be more than the average company will spend on publicizing itself ever again.

The only advice I can give to directors of companies coming to the market is that they should have a much greater ability to say no to the PR advice than we had. For example, the new corporate video, whose main purpose was to be shown to the meetings of institutional investors, was rarely used. It was played while the investors were being shown to their seats. Our brokers believed that corporate videos were anathema to analysts and investors alike. The corporate brochure, because of legal complications, was not provided in time for the NFC flotation. Many investors have commented that they preferred the old-style annual report – although the rather stylish report prepared for the flotation did win an industry award. It appealed, it seems, to other PR men. If we were floating companies every year we would soon find what is necessary and cost effective – but because flotation is a one-off exercise, we were not in a position to know any different at the time.

The advisers were therefore assembled. All of them work long hours and immensely hard, the adrenalin flows, the excitement grows, and so does the cost. In the case of NFC coming to the market by way of an introduction and a rights issue to raise £50m of new money *not* underwritten cost £6.3m. Another way to look at it is that NFC now owed £6.3m more to the banks. At interest rates of around 14 per cent, earnings have been reduced by £600,000 per annum. I wonder whether the new investors, given the choice, would have preferred rather less protection in exchange for rather more earnings per share. In the case of Community Hospitals, a company capitalized today at around £50m, it cost £1.5m to raise £18.5m of new money. The same thought must apply. To this must be added at least a similar cost of the management time involved.

Is there a better solution? It is difficult to present one when government is hell bent on demanding greater and greater protection for the investor. It is doubly difficult to recommend less costly diligence when the Guinness and County NatWest scandals are fresh in investors' minds. But the question still must be posed to the investor: does he really want the protection at the price it is costing him? John Gunn, the dynamic Chairman of British &

Commonwealth Holdings, the financial services group, has recently stated that compliance with the new investor protection rules was costing his investors over £2m per annum. This is the cost to but one City company. Multiplied by all the firms covered by the Financial Services Act (1986), the investors are paying a heavy but unquantifiable price for their protection, and even then the protection is not absolute. It does not guarantee the end of share frauds, insider dealing or the misleading of the market. The fundamental problem is that the person who pays the bill (the investor) is never asked whether the protection he is getting is worth the cost, unlike a burglar alarm or an insurance policy where each individual can decide whether the security it gives is really worth the cost he is paying.

With new share issues there is no cost champion of the consumer (in this case, the investor in the new shares). The Stock Exchange is not itself the guardian of the costs of bringing the company to market. The more work the sponsor, the lawyers and the accountants have to do, the higher the fees that can be justified. The PR firms in part are rewarded from the level of advertising and promotional spend. All work well and conscientiously, but no one is really safeguarding the total cost except the company who is being confronted with a one-off experience, and therefore has to rely on whatever advice is given. The net effect of all this is that the cost of coming to market has reached unrealistic levels.

My solution is simple. A company seeking to have its shares quoted should engage in a straight negotiation between itself and the Stock Exchange. There should be no intermediary or sponsor. The offer document to shareholders should be drawn up in simple language that the wider share-owning public can understand. It would not be a document prepared by City people for City people. The financial facts would be accepted without further investigation from the audited accounts of the company, providing the accounts had not been qualified by the auditors. The 'long form' report would be eliminated. This might increase the risk of someone losing money as a result of investing in a less than fully authenticated company. To balance this risk every company seeking a listing would be required to contribute to a central insurance fund; say, 1 per cent of the new money to be raised. The Stock Exchange would administer such a fund. Any genuine claims from aggrieved investors would be paid out of the fund. This may seem to be trivializing the issue, but this is the way the holiday industry faced up to loss of customers' confidence in the industry due to the number of tour operators going out of business. First-class cheap insurance is now available to protect the traveller against the misfeasance of any travel operator or retailer.

The requirement to advertise the full prospectus in the media should be dropped. It should be up to the company how it advertises the fact that its shares will be available for trading. Finally, no pressure would be put on the company to have its issue underwritten. The directors of the company should judge whether it could afford the risk of failure of the issue. These proposals would radically simplify the process of bringing a company to market. It would make the offering more easily understood by the general public. It would reduce the horrendous costs.

NFC now had to decide *how* it should come to the market given the mandate we had had from our shareholders, and bearing in mind the employee ownership culture we wanted to preserve. Our objectives were clear: to obtain a share value and market rating higher than our competitors, to raise some new money to reduce the debt in the business, and to try to persuade our existing shareholders not to sell their shares on flotation, in this way retaining family and employee control.

The computer model built by Philip Roe, which simulated how rich we could make new employees, was also able to analyse the proportion of the voting rights that would be held by differing groups given various assumptions. The most critical factor was the pace at which the existing family shareholders sold their shares. If they sold at the rate of 20 per cent per annum, family control, even with the double voting rights, disappeared within four years. On the other hand, profit-sharing was critical in recycling shares into employee ownership. We developed a scenario against which we could formulate our flotation plans.

If the family sold less than 10 per cent of their shares per annum, if profits grew sufficiently for us to allocate 15 per cent of pre-tax profits a year for profit-sharing, if at least 55 per cent of the employees saved under the share-saving scheme, if we were frugal in issuing new shares for acquisitions, and if we retained the double voting right for employees, we could still be family-controlled and in a stable state as we entered the twenty-first century.

Our advisers drew up a list of the possible ways for NFC to come to the market. Their preference was for the normal 'offer for sale' route. This meant there would be an agreed amount of shares made available for sale to the new shareholders at a pre-fixed price. This was the route that most privatizations had travelled. It had one major disadvantage for us. The existing shareholders would be asked in advance to commit themselves to the number of shares they would sell on flotation so that they could be bundled together with new shares being issued. The purpose of this is to create an orderly market. Our message to the shareholders was to be 'Don't sell if you value employee control'. The offer for sale route did not therefore find favour. It presented a confusing message to the shareholders. 'How many shares do you want to sell? Please don't sell any.'

Our sponsors BZW came up with an alternative plan that I, for one, had never heard of. It is called an 'introduction to the stock market'. This merely allows the market makers to start dealing in your shares from an agreed date. There is no preordained issue price – the price of the shares is solely determined by the market trading of your shares at the time of the flotation. In order to go down this route, in the first place a substantial number of shareholders must already exist – no problem for us, as we by this time had over forty thousand. Secondly, the market is not asked to subscribe for a significant amount of new money. This might have caused us a problem as we wished to raise perhaps £50m to £100m, but we cleared the potential obstacle quite easily: we would first offer the opportunity to buy new shares to our existing shareholders by way of a rights issue. A rights issue is the usual way of raising new money once a company is on the stock market. It is a little strange for a company coming to market for the first time. Our cash flows were proving to be much stronger than we forecast, so the need to raise anywhere near the £100m ceiling was reducing daily. In the event we decided we could manage with £50m.

The benefits of the introduction, coupled with a rights issue, gradually emerged. For example, when we were considering at what price we should issue the new shares, like a blinding flash the realization came to us that if we issued the new shares at a very low price, it would have two effects. Those existing shareholders who wanted to buy more shares could obtain them at a low price, and this would encourage them to take up their rights. Those who were just waiting for the flotation to sell some shares and get a little cash into their hands would be able to do so without necessarily selling any of their base load of shares. The 'rights' that they would be given to buy shares at a low price could be sold at the full market price once the NFC was introduced to the stock market and its shares were quoted and being traded. As a spin-off from making the rights issue price low, we did not need to have the issue underwritten since there was no risk of the new shares not being bought. This saved us 2 per cent of the underwriting costs.

After many hours of discussion and debate with our advisers, and with our eyes firmly on our mission statement of retaining employee control, we arrived at a unique route to flotation. We would come to the market by way of an introduction preceded by a £50m rights issue. For each eight shares held by an existing shareholder, one additional share at £1.30 each would be offered. We thought when the shares were quoted they would be priced at about £2.10, so we were offering an 80p discount. In fact the share price post-flotation settled in the range of 230p–260p. If the average shareholder who invested £700 in 1982 sold his rights rather than retained them, he would receive a cheque for more than £2800. This, we felt, should be enough to make sure that the existing investors did not sell too many of their base load.

The advisers were always concerned that too much innovation would cause suspicion among the institutions, who tended to be conservative, and that they would then downgrade the value of the shares. On the contrary, I felt instinctively that most investors liked to see some difference, uniqueness and invention in the management of the companies they supported. If anything, innovation would make them value the company higher. Which of us was right would only be known after the shares had been floated. One unique feature was never in doubt: all the advisers recognized that we had to have the double voting rights for employees. They worked hard and enthusiastically to make sure that we got it.

Neither the Stock Exchange nor the two powerful investor protection groups like voting structures that give one class of share more votes than another. In reality, though, many companies listed on the Stock Exchange have special voting rights attached to certain classes of shares. In some cases the minority shareholders have been able to frustrate the will of the majority because of those differential voting rights. The most famous ongoing saga is the Savoy Group, where Trusthouse Forte have the majority of the shares but not the majority of the voting rights. They have so far been frustrated in their attempt to take control of the company. Mind you, THF cannot complain too much as it has a variable voting structure which in turn protects it from takeover. The major worry of the institutions is that special voting rights can result in the protection of an inefficient management.

We came at double voting rights from the other end of the argument. We believed that the way companies are taken over, split up and sold off without any consideration of the wishes of the employees is a modern-day anachronism. Indeed it should not be allowed to survive into the next century. Company law was changed some thirty years ago to require directors to take into account in their decisions not only the interests of the owners (the shareholders) but also the interests of the employees. We felt that it was time that owners had the same requirement laid upon them. Before selling they should be required to listen to the voices of the employees. Furthermore, I believe that as the European Community develops, the UK will be isolated, unless it finds a British way forward on employee rights. The employees' demand to contribute to the decisions that affect their working life will only become more strident. It will have the support of the rest of the EEC, and the UK will have to come to terms with it. Nothing is as important to any worker as a change of ownership. If we could establish a UK vision of industrial democracy that gave employee shareholders special rights on takeovers and other major decisions, this might be an acceptable form of employee involvement as far as the EEC is concerned.

We believed employee double voting rights would be good not only for the NFC, but also for the UK as it wrestles with the problems of industrial democracy posed by the Common Market. We sought to emphasize the generality of our case. Our streetwise advisers suggested that we should mute its general application and make the case to the Stock Exchange of the uniqueness of NFC that it would not be creating a precedent which could be readily followed by others.

I suspect they were right. It did not take the Stock Exchange long to accept that NFC was a special case. After all, we were the pioneers in employee ownership and were strong players in the wider share ownership movement that the Council of the Stock Exchange was pledged to support.

The problem lay in the mechanism which we wanted to use to get there, which caused the inordinate length of time it took to get approval for the double voting rights. We wanted a predator to have to firmly declare his intentions when he had accumulated only 8 per cent of the shares. The requirement of the takeover code is that a predator can acquire 29.9 per cent of the equity of the target company before he has to make his intention known and make a bid. We wanted the outcome of the bid to be determined by all the shareholders voting in general meeting, having been presented with the arguments in advance. The Stock Exchange preferred the normal system where, in a takeover, shareholder acceptances trickle in over a fair length of time, which means that deals can be done between the predator and the key shareholders along the way. Although we were not wishing to change the world, we did believe that our system would be a fairer system for all shareholders than the rules of the current takeover code. The predator, by being able to buy such a large proportion of the total shares before he makes his final offer, is frequently able to buy the company relatively cheaply, and often to the disadvantage of the less-knowledgeable shareholders who sell first.

Finally, we wanted the double voting rights for the employees only to come into play on the one issue of takeover. The Stock

Exchange were prepared to offer a compromise. The deal was that if we would drop the 8 per cent trigger point, they would agree to double voting right applying to all issues that required shareholder approval. The deal gave power to the employees over more issues, but it did not allow us the debate and a general vote if a takeover was attempted.

Negotiating with the Stock Exchange is an unusual experience. The admission of a company to a full listing is the responsibility of the New Issues Committee. They prefer not to be involved directly with the applicant company. The admission is handled by the stockbrokers with the officials who serve on the committee. Our application raised such fundamental issues for employee ownership that I felt it was sensible to have an informal discussion with the main decision takers of the committee, the Chairman and Deputy Chairman. I suggested a discussion over lunch. In the commercial world this is how most of the difficult problems are sorted out. They preferred an 'informal' discussion at the Stock Exchange. The informal discussion turned out to involve not just the Chairman and Deputy Chairman, but one or two other members of the committee plus all the relevant Stock Exchange permanent staff. It proved to be as informal a discussion as attending a banquet at the Guildhall is an informal dinner. I made a statement, questions were asked, the meeting was closed. There was no negotiation, little exploration of possible compromise – or, if we gave this, would you concede that? The negotiating reverted to the Stock Exchange officials and Phillips & Drew, from which I was excluded. It was all very frustrating.

After yet more weeks after which no decision had emerged, we eventually requested a formal meeting with the committee. We were awarded a thirty-minute slot. We made our presentation again, which was courteously received. We were questioned by the full committee which was only one or two larger than the informal group. The Chairman finished by thanking us and reminding us that the decision of his committee on listing of a company was final, and there was nowhere else we could go on appeal. Marianne Burton, the tenacious, charming but tough-minded executive of Phillips & Drew who was looking after our passage to the market, warned me in advance that however strongly I felt it would do our cause no good by getting angry. The committee had their way of doing things and I just had to accept it. But the Chairman's final remark irked me and I had to respond. I reminded him that NFC was an international company and that if the London Stock Exchange was not prepared to support our form of employee share ownership, there were other stock markets in Europe and indeed in New York who would. I am sure the outburst did our cause no good, but at least it made me feel better.

So behind closed doors the deal was struck. The way was now clear to take NFC to the stock market, and it was substantially the way we had proposed and our shareholders had authorized. Two months of intensive communication followed, firstly with our existing shareholders. They had to understand exactly what the rights issue and the introduction of NFC to the Stock Exchange meant for them. We held ten large meetings around the UK in January 1989. They were well attended despite being held on Sunday mornings. One of the meetings I took was in west London. We had booked a hotel near Heathrow airport and had calculated that no more than 750 would attend. In the event twice that number turned up – they were standing all round the hall and squatting in the aisles. The same was true in many of the other locations in other parts of the country addressed by my colleagues. The interest was intense.

This communication exercise was not only happening all over the UK but also in the USA, Australia, New Zealand and Singapore where we had operations and employee shareholders. It was a complex series of messages that we had to put over. We had to explain the rights issue; how they could buy and sell shares in the future. The continuing role of the share trust for the small shareholder and the mysteries of 'tail swallowing' were revealed. By 'tail swallowing' you can sell some of the rights and use the cash you receive to buy the balance. In this way an existing shareholder finishes up with more shares without having to find any additional cash. We felt many would be interested in this procedure. We also wanted to shout loud and clear that this was not only about how they could make the most money by share manipulation. It was the time when the future of NFC's unique employee and family control was passed into their hands to do with as they thought best. If they valued that concept, they would be long-term investors and be prudent in their future selling of shares. If the concept meant nothing to them, they would sell their shares and walk away with the cash.

We had to get this ownership message over without giving *investment* advice. As we were not approved financial advisers registered with any of the agencies controlled by the Securities and Investments Commission, we would be on the wrong side of the law if we gave investment advice. At the EGM held to agree the new articles for the company before flotation, one of the old pensioners stood up and said, 'Sir Peter, we have followed the board and your advice for more than eight years and you haven't let us down yet. All this Stock Exchange stuff and prospectuses confuses me at ninety-two years of age. Will you just tell me what to do?'

The front two rows of the meeting were full of lawyers. 'I can't answer that question,' I replied. 'It would be against the law to advise you as I am not licensed as a financial adviser.'

The old family member rose slowly again to his feet. 'If that's what the law says, it's bloody daft.'

He has a point – it echoes my concern about the cost and wisdom of so much shareholder protection. There is little doubt that if employee share ownership is to flourish, the leaders of businesses will have to be allowed to give advice to their employees about share purchase.

We took the line that we were *not* giving financial advice, but pointing out the result of their action, not upon the value of the shares, but upon the ownership and control of the NFC. If collectively they did not take up any of their rights and sold more than 10 per cent of their existing holding, within five years the NFC family would no longer have control over its own destiny. Again I was able to tell them that the board and I were leading from the front. The majority of us promised the shareholders that we would be taking up a substantial part of our rights and were committed not to sell more than 10 per cent of our base load of shares in any year. Many left the meetings in thoughtful mood. Many came to the rostrum and said they were wholeheartedly behind us. It is always the ones that quietly depart home without saying anything that you have to worry about.

We also had to address the potential buyers of NFC shares once we were introduced to the Stock Exchange. The first group to tackle were the people who, it is said, influence the investors: the analysts and the media. Each of the major stockbrokers has an analyst who specializes in transport and shipping stock, and it was in this section of the market that NFC would be classified. One of the reasons we chose Phillips & Drew and Kitcat & Aitken as our brokers was because they had two of the most respected transport analysts working for them – Richard Hannah and Allan Kelsey. We had to ensure that the key group of analysts really did understand the company. In particular, that they were clear about the markets we were in, how we operated in these markets, and the extent to which we dominated them.

We therefore spent time briefing the analysts so that when they came to write their reports on the NFC they would not misadvise because they had misunderstood. In the event they were embarrassingly complimentary about the NFC, its management and its strategies. Some were even prepared to argue that our quirks – the double voting rights and generous profit-sharing – were justified because superior employee motivation in a service industry gave marketing edge.

We did not neglect the press or television. They had supported our concepts and values for the eight years since the buy-out. They did not desert us as we came to flotation. Bob Head, the industrial editor of the *Mirror*, gave the shares a three-star rating (their highest) with the single comment, 'Great'. The *Financial Weekly* came out with an in-depth analysis of the company and gave us a five-star rating. We were only the fourth company to get such a rating in over 250 appraisals they had done. They put us alongside Sainsbury's, Glaxo and Hanson Trust, believing our employee focus could well set the trend for successful companies in the 1990s. But as ever the main issue the media homed in on was speculation over the opening price. The highest forecast of the most bullish journalist in the event proved to be 30p too low.

We then sought to influence the institutional investors at a series of meetings, mainly over lunch and dinner arranged by our two stockbrokers. Jack Mather, James Watson and I sacrificed our stomachs and our figures in the interests of the NFC.

195

In the words of Philip Mayo at the 1989 AGM in Brighton, 'They ate their way to victory.' It was always a team presentation: Jack Mather, the Chief Executive, concentrated on the business issues, James Watson, the Deputy Chairman, talked them through the financial statements, and I had to convince the investors that our unique values would give market edge. I even demonstrated that profit-sharing to the employees was good for them as investors. Our version of profit-sharing, because it was performance-related, meant that in the short term significant variations of operating profit each year would be smoothed out by the time they reached the earnings per share line. If, for example, operating profits in any one year dropped by 10 per cent, this reduction would be entirely absorbed by the profit-sharing scheme so that earnings per share would not fall at all. A company producing stable earnings is always more attractive and should command a better price than a company with volatile earnings. I *think*, but I cannot be sure, that I convinced them.

We also set out to show that NFC had quality management in depth and was not a one-man band. The media often seeks to 'personalize' companies to one individual – it makes for simpler imagery. Hanson Trust, if you believe the media, is all about James Hanson. BTR is Owen Green, ICI was John Harvey-Jones, Heron is Gerald Ronson. The reality is that all these companies have to have a depth of management below the figurehead for them to be any good. We invited all investors to our depots to meet the next layer of management – we wanted our new investors to know what our employee investors have no doubt about: NFC is far from being just Peter Thompson.

We were also anxious that the available shares did not all fall into the hands of the large institutions. We actively wooed a number of the regional and private client brokers so that they in turn could interest their clients in the shares. The one group of investors we did not reach satisfactorily was the mass of small investors who had only ever invested in the privatization stocks – British Telecom, British Gas, and so on. While this group represents the many thousands of investors who had never held shares before, and are therefore the Thatcher army of popular capitalists, most of them have never bought any other shares and have not become regular and active investors. We did not really find a way to give them any special treatment, although we did want them to invest. The problem was that a definite number of shares at a fixed price per share was not being offered. The number of shares available depended upon whether the existing shareholders took up their rights or sold. The price would only be fixed when trading started on the Stock Exchange. All we could do for these 'long-term Sids', as we affectionately called them after the character in the successful British Gas flotation campaign, was to publicize through the press the telephone number of a low-cost share dealing service. If they wished to be involved with NFC shares they had to become active investors and use a stockbroker. I do not believe many of them used the service. If wider share ownership is to be achieved, this group of 'Sids' must be encouraged to become active investors and users of the stock market.

Our campaign did not have the dramatic centre piece enjoyed by most large companies or nationalized industries when they go to the market, and there could be no hype surrounding the price at which the shares were to be offered, since in our case the first day of trading would determine the price at which the shares were selling. Not for us the SAS abseiling down the office tower, unfurling the price as they go, nor the fleet of hot air balloons with the magic number on the side. Nor was there the television coverage of the would-be investors dashing to hand over their application for shares at the last minute on the closing day. Nor the announcement of the extent of the oversubscription and the much-heralded decision of the directors on who will get what by their allocation of shares. Not even the publicity of the arrest of prominent citizens seeking to have too many bites of the allocation apple by multi-applications!

Our drama was lower key and revolved around the happenings on the morning of 6 February, the date that our shares would first be traded. Phillips & Drew, being the lead stockbroker, was also the lead market maker and our excitement was centred on the activities in their dealing room. Our fortunes were being orchestrated by Steve Dalby, a slightly overweight but youthful East Ender with the quicksilver numeracy I had only previously observed in the book-making fraternity. We were all invited to have breakfast at Phillips & Drew's office, along with countless members of the press and two television crews. We had also invited along three of our worker shareholders from our London depots. They would share in the excitement and also, we hoped, give 'human-interest' interviews for the next day's morning papers.

At 7.45 a.m. we went on to the dealing floor where there was a buzz of activity. Although the market makers were putting a cool professional face on it all, I suspect it was something new for them. They had not handled very many major companies coming to the market by means of an introduction. They had to judge the opening price. The usual information about the size of the oversubscription, which gives some kind of an indication of the level of demand at the offer price, was not available. They had to judge the price from the activities of the salesmen who had been busy among the institutions trying to assess the level of demand at varying market prices. Rumours abounded, being fanned by at least one of the more aggressive young salesmen who claimed he had orders for the whole of the rights issue at £2.40. It was clearly a difficult transaction to price as the market makers themselves had little previous experience of this kind of flotation. The general view of the business editors of the newspapers was that the shares would settle at somewhere between £2.00 and £2.20. Even at this price it would mean that the city was rating NFC at least 40 per cent higher than its competitors – despite the double voting rights and the profit-sharing. At 7.50 a.m. the chief market maker announced the price over the loudspeakers: NFC – 225/230. They would buy at 225 and sell at 230. The price went on the dealing screens.

I was standing in front of a TV camera and was conducting a live interview for BBC. I managed to stutter that I was delighted at the opening price and how it showed that the City had recognized the commercial advantages of NFC employee-focused values. While this three-minute interview was going on behind me the price of the shares was moving about like the lights of a one-armed bandit about to deliver the jackpot. Within twenty minutes the buying price rose to 265 with the selling price at 270. One of the market makers had got out of step so that his buying price was actually higher than the other dealers' selling price. The other market makers pounced and he quickly adjusted to get himself back in the pack. Steve was jotting down on his pad all the bargains which had been struck, controlling his stock position minute by minute and commanding, to the last 20,000 shares, the young dealers working on the screens.

I remember as a boy being amazed when watching semi-literate farm workers play darts – how they could, in a split second, carry out the most complex calculations of exactly which doubles or trebles they needed to finish. The dealing team (while far from semi-literate) had the same feel for numbers. In the midst of it all, I asked Steve how much he had made or lost on the trading so far – £750,000 gain flashed back the answer while he authorized three more deals.

The excitement was infectious. There were two jokers in the pack. Would there be any shares available? What would be the top buying price of the regional brokers who were mainly satisfying the demands of the private investors? BZW helped to make the market by supplying shares into the early dealings. They were overcommitted to NFC shares and had told us it was their intention to reduce their holding from a little over 8 per cent to below 5 per cent. As far as we could gather, there were a large number of orders from the regional brokers with instructions to buy at best. But the big battalions were also coming in. I was pleased to see that Postel were buying. They were the pension fund which needed persuasion that our double voting shares were justified. As a general policy they did not buy variable voting right shares; obviously they had been persuaded that NFC was a special case.

The first thirty minutes of hectic dealing was followed by the kind of photographic sessions that the media love. The three worker shareholders gathered around a dealing screen listening to my words of wisdom. They lifted me on to their shoulders – although I must say they made a pretty poor fist of it. I can only assume that good living had made them out of condition. Inevitably, a picture was taken of the three of them sitting in the cocktail lounge of the Waldorf surrounded by potted palms drinking a glass of champagne – bought, I hasten to add, by the photographer. It was all great fun and a wealth of good photographs appeared in the papers the next day. By midday the price had settled at around 260 and we returned to Bedford, where we had a celebration party with all the staff. Similar parties were breaking out all over NFC.

The next day was the time for cool reflection. We had come to the market in triumph; we had been given a much higher rating than I had anticipated. I felt a price–earning ratio of 16 would be a fair reflection of our quality. We had been given a PE of over 18. We had before the flotation tried to define what we meant by success. We all agreed success was not about getting the highest possible opening price. It was about having a price that we could live with, which would gradually increase in line with our expected increase of earnings per share. The nightmare for us would be to experience the sort of market treatment that Richard Branson's company Virgin received. When Virgin was first quoted, it reached a price of 140p per share. As a result of Black Monday and other factors, the price collapsed to around 80p where it stubbornly stayed, despite all the efforts of the management team. Eventually Richard Branson felt the only way out was to buy back the shares from his colleagues and supporters whom he felt had been let down and to take the company private.

To ensure employee shareholders were long-term investors, we knew we needed a steadily rising share price associated with generous dividends. We gave them generous dividends when we came to the market, and increased our dividends by 75 per cent, thus signalling that we intended to be a company which wanted its shareholders to receive a significant proportion of the profits in the form of dividends. We were not going to be in the league of companies that held on to their profits rather than distribute them. We believed if our dividends were 2½ times covered by profits, this was a reasonable situation.

The very high share price was a worry. We thought the price reflected two things: the expectation of the market about our future performance, but also the scarcity of stock available. A scarcity premium had clearly crept in. It meant that at the current level of the stock market it would take perhaps six to nine months of good performance to move the share price significantly higher than the opening price. It would need our family share-holders to keep faith in what was an unusual situation for them. They faced a period of some months when the share price would remain fairly static. In the meantime we would maintain their confidence by continuing to report on results each quarter and continuing to give the 'best view' of the board of the expected out-turn for the year. Despite all the work involved in the flotation, the business was still trading well and the forward view was as encouraging as ever. But the fact was that from the beginning the shares were being traded at a full price on the market.

Final decisions on the rights issue did not have to be taken for three weeks. In every household our shareholders were debating what each of them should be doing with their shares. We at the centre had the slow agony of waiting for at least three months before we could know the outcome of all those decisions. It would take the registrar at least three months before he could give us a print out of the new share register. Only then would we be able to judge how they had behaved. Had they taken up their rights or had they all sold? Had they sold a large part of their base holdings or were they still there?

10

Will it Survive?

'What we've essentially said [to employees]
is that the future of the business rests with
you guys.'
                    Investors Chronicle, 18 August 1989

Will NFC's people-focused values survive, and will its employee control remain intact following its flotation on the stock market? In addition, will the management philosophies and values, which we have sought by example to offer to the business world as a means of employee motivation, survive? Perhaps this latter is the more important issue. What chance is there that these management philosophies, which we hold so dear, will be adopted by industry at large?

The heart of our belief is that a participative, communicative, sharing, employee-focused management will produce better results than an authoritarian management. The style is not an end in itself – although a thesis could be developed that, as a way of increasing human satisfaction and happiness, it is worth pursuing for its own sake. My argument is limited to the hard commercial case that in a service industry, this style of management is more likely to deliver superior customer service than any other. In a service industry this is the marketing edge that a business needs if it is to outperform its competitors.

The best UK businesses recognize this, and to a greater or lesser extent practise parts of the NFC philosophy. For example, in the last ten years much progress has been made in communication with and informing staff. Even this progress needed a catalyst. I believe this came from the deal which David Steel struck with

James Callaghan as the price of the Liberal Party being prepared to support the minority Labour government following the hung parliament in 1974. As part of the deal for the formation of the Lib/Lab pact, legislation was passed which required all companies to state in their annual reports to their shareholders what action they had taken to communicate with their employees during the year. Even the most fossilized chairman was reluctant to have to say that his company had done nothing.

Most companies today prepare special annual reports for employees, many have developed good day-to-day communication networks – often adopting the briefing group technique. For over twenty-five years, under the charismatic and committed leadership of John Garnett, the Industrial Society campaigned for better communication. In one form or another the briefing group concept that they pioneered has been widely adopted by industry. In its simplest form it means that at every workplace the staff are regularly called together to be told what is going on. The better companies welcome feedback and challenge to the decisions that are being communicated. The authoritarian companies are happy to report to their shareholders annually that the workers have been well and truly told! I know of no company chairman nowadays who would confess to practising the mushroom philosophy of management – keep them in the dark and occasionally throw them some bullshit! Even if some still adopt it as a management style, they would no longer admit to it.

The better companies recognize that the way to obtain commitment goes far beyond mere communication. It has to embrace involvement; in decision taking, in financial sharing. The Industrial Society itself under its new leader Alistair Graham, who came from a trade union background, recognized the need to talk less about briefing groups (with hints of one-way communication) and more about participation (which is all about real involvement). Their own policy document 'The Blueprint for Success', to which many industrialists contributed, points the new way forward. So the concept of involvement is being widely adopted, whether through quality circles, which is the Japanese way of bringing the collective muscle and minds of the workforce to bear on product improvement, or active suggestion schemes which is a more British approach. We tend to prefer the quiet, thoughtful, individual contribution.

As yet, the growth in participation in micro decisions has rarely spread into involvement in macro decisions. Few business leaders recognize the rights of the employee to make a contribution to the broad future strategy of the company. I know of no company other than NFC where the workforce was invited to have its say in the discussion about selling the company before the decision was finally made. But there are one or two signs about that workforces are becoming less compliant. They are showing less willingness to be treated as commodities which can be traded at the whims of the owners.

In recent years two examples come to mind of employees' voices demanding to be heard on takeovers. The first was the sale proposed by the government of the Land Rover Company to General Motors. The employees, led by active trade union officers, were extremely vocal in opposing the takeover. They came out loud and clear in favour of an employee-management buy-out, and, through Unity Bank (the trade-union-formed bank), were prepared to help finance the deal. The combination of a vigorous political campaign plus worker opposition was enough to frustrate the takeover. But it must be said that it was the government, obviously more susceptible to political pressure, who were influenced not to sell.

The next example, which went the other way, was in the Nestlé/Rowntree takeover battle. The Rowntree board were adamant that the Nestlé bid should be rejected. At a critical stage the representatives of the workforce were called together by their union officials. To everyone's surprise, the advice that came out of the meeting to the board of Rowntrees was that it was in the best interests of the workforce and the company for positive negotiation with Nestlé to take place. One must wonder whether the Rowntree workforce had been involved by the management in the decisions of the company in the past. It seems hard to believe that a committed workforce would have delivered such a body blow to the independence of their company.

I believe that the days of workforces succumbing to imposed changes of ownership are numbered. This is inevitable, as employees reach ever higher educational standards, as popular share ownership grows, and as industry adopts participative management as the way to improve service and product standards. In this environment owners cannot expect the employees to remain docile about the most important decision of all: who they are owned by.

Political forces are also at work. The European Community is determined to push through some kind of social charter which will give to employees the right of involvement in the key decisions of their companies. Most countries in the EEC are happy to pass legislation which gives workers representative rights at board level. After all, the supervisory board structure, introduced by the British when they occupied Germany after the war, has in no way hindered the industrial advance of West Germany. On the contrary many would argue that the involvement of the workers has been a positive force which has had a major part to play in the excellent industrial relations of that country. Yet British industry stands like Horatio on the bridge, repelling the successive attempts of the Bullock report in the 1960s, and the Vredeling initiative in the early 1980s, to make boards more representative of the views of the workforce.

In 1987 I was invited to chair one of the CBI's most important committees – the Employment Policy Committee. Of course, I was flattered, but before accepting I had a long discussion with the then President and the Director General. Both men held liberal views on employee involvement. We shared many common values. However, when I said that if voluntary progress was not forthcoming in involving employees in decision-taking at board level, I would welcome legislation to hasten the process, our paths diverged. Whatever their personal views, they were adamant that this was one of the sacred cows that the directors of British industry would not have slaughtered.

So in the UK, any advance in social contract legislation is opposed, and nothing is offered as an alternative. Perhaps a British alternative could lie in the realms of employee shareholding.

There have been major advances in wider share ownership in the UK since the advent of the Thatcher government. The number of individuals owning shares has quadrupled, mainly as a result of the privatization programmes. Similarly, and helped by tax breaks that have made a variety of employee-share schemes financially attractive, many more workers own either options or shares in the companies for which they work. This tide is flowing strongly and I have no doubt that within a decade it will be the rule rather than the exception for employees to have a capital stake in their own company. As ever there is more that the Chancellor of the Exchequer could do to encourage this. The employee stock ownership programmes that are widespread in the USA have much more federal tax support than our schemes in the UK. The signs are that there will be some movement by the UK government to improve the tax incentives over the next few years. So the quantum of company shares owned by the employees should continue to grow fast.

I do not see much signs of progress, however, towards boards of directors wishing to treat their employees as special shareholders. UK business does not seem to want to adopt the NFC philosophy that an individual who has invested his life and his money in a company should have special rights over the individual who only invests his money. One share, one vote is still the market creed, and also the sentiment of most boards of directors. Even though there is no groundswell to encourage differential voting rights, I would have hoped to have seen more positive efforts by companies to make their employee shareholders feel that they are special. At the least, more companies should be encouraging their employees to attend the annual general meeting. They also should take steps to make the AGM a significant event in the company calendar. It should be the occasion on which the directors truly do report on their stewardship of the company. Employees should be encouraged to question their directors closely about the business, instead of being actively discouraged from asking questions, or even attending, as is often the case. I am afraid it will be many years before companies make the same effort to involve their employee shareholders in corporate strategy as they do to ensure that major institutional shareholders understand it.

During the Thatcher years, there has been much growth of personal capital. The taxation system has allowed and encouraged it. The enterprise culture has also helped. Many people today have disposable capital in excess of £250,000. Indeed, the

NFC alone has created more than five hundred of this growing happy band. But in the main, large companies have tended to concentrate their efforts in private capital building on the top management team. Share options are normally confined to the few. Not much imagination has been applied to trying to build worthwhile capital stakes for all employees. The main stake that most individuals have is locked up in their company pension schemes. They regard this, and indeed are encouraged to do so, not as a capital sum but as a source of future income.

I would like to think that, as our form of social contract, the UK might tender to the EEC a package which offers to each worker involvement in the policy direction of his company through positive programmes of creating worker capitalists. The programmes would include: profit-sharing in shares (at least 10 per cent of pre-tax profits); preferential voting rights for employees; special employee policy and strategy meetings; and, on the key issue of ultimate ownership, the employees to have the right to vote a golden share which might represent up to one-third of the voting rights of all shareholders. This programme, if coupled with meaningful AGMs and regular shareholder meetings while avoiding any commitment to employee representation at board level, would mean that boards of directors would become more accountable for their actions not just to their shareholders, but also to their employees.

Perhaps the greatest disappointment to me has been how few companies have followed the NFC lead in employee ownership. Yet there has been a quiet revolution taking place in the ownership of companies. Management buy-outs and buy-ins have flourished. In the last five years alone, the value of this kind of takeover has exceeded £12 billion and the number of companies involved is more than 1500. Each of these companies could have gone down the employee-ownership route – very few have. Many have pointed to this fact as being the NFC's Achilles heel. If you are so good, they say, why have so few followed?

In the absence of any real research, I can only surmise. I suggest it is a dislike of, or even fear of, the necessary management style, coupled with my own motivational friend, greed. Running an employee-owned business is for many an uncomfortable management task. Why should you submit yourself to constant examination of your actions by your workforce, and why be accountable to them? Much easier just to convince a handful of your director colleagues that your actions are acceptable. The other side of the same coin is that if the management buy-out is successful, the success has to be shared among fewer people and hence the privileged few become richer. These arguments I understand only too well. I can only counter them with the fact that at least our company has been successful beyond anyone's wildest dreams by following the employee involvement route. It has created many millionaires who have enough wealth to meet their needs and who have the added satisfaction that they have shared their success and fortune with thousands of others. This argument may not, I suppose, convince the aggressive entrepreneurs who tend to lead management buy-outs. Perhaps we need some additional tax incentives to be offered to genuine employee buy-outs, so that greed as well as altruism can be satisfied.

All is not lost. In the last two years there are signs that other employee buy-outs are happening. For example, the privatiz-ation of the bus industry produced a handful. If we held a meeting of all the boards of employee-owned businesses, we would not yet fill the Albert Hall, but at least we are too many to be accommodated in a telephone booth. Despite the slow progress, I do believe that in a decade from now there will be a significant and growing number of employee-controlled companies in the UK. But there again, I have always been an optimist!

From all this I conclude that many of the values that NFC embraces will take root and flourish. An increasingly well-educated workforce will demand communication, involvement and sharing in the wealth that they are creating. In an ever-more competitive market, it is the companies that can attract and retain first-class people that will succeed. I have little doubt that our values will not only survive but prosper to the point where they are the norm in British industry.

For this to happen there will also have to be a marked change in the attitudes of the institutional investor. On the whole, the investor protection societies see profit-sharing, share options and differential voting rights for employees as a means of reducing the value of the equity owned by the institution, and as such they need to be carefully policed and limited in extent. Their 'rules' are clear enough. No more than 5 per cent of total equity to be offered to management for share options. No more than 5 per cent of UK-earned profit to be allocated for profit-sharing amongst UK employees. Differential voting rights are to be discouraged.

These rules need relaxing, but that relaxation will only happen if companies such as NFC, who came to the market without these 'rules', show that they can perform better than companies which adhere to the rules. In the short term, because there are so few of us, this is going to be difficult to prove. What is needed is a number of agreed experiments. A single company in each sector might be chosen. The directors of that company would have to demonstrate to the investor protection groups that they are committed to employee involvement. Any concessions which are granted would be used primarily to spread share ownership over a wide base of employees, rather than using the concessions to boost the options and share ownership of the few top managers. After five years an evaluation could then be made of the relative success in their sectors of the chosen companies. I believe that these companies would have outperformed their competitors. The concessions would have created additional shareholder value rather than diminishing it. A short-term reduction in earnings per share as a result of a more generous profit-sharing scheme would prove to be like capital investment. Not capital investment in plant or machinery which everyone applauds, but capital investment in motivation which most regard with great suspicion.

This of course requires a sea change in the attitudes of the investor protection groups. But, even more, it requires a change in the attitudes of much of UK senior management. It requires them to recognize that success is not only about good strategies and good decisions. It is also about employees welcoming those decisions because they have been involved in the process of decision-making. It requires managements to be less greedy about taking the lion's share of the available share options and profit-sharing, and to set themselves targets not only for building their own personal wealth but also for building the wealth of their employees. If every business set itself the target that, given success of the company, within ten years its share motivation package would build a capital stake in the company for each employee of twice their current annual wage or salary, I know that the performance of such companies would be transformed.

Many chief executives are proud of their short-term incentive programmes. They boast about the bonus-earning possibilities of their salesmen, operatives or management. Rarely do I hear of similar plans to boost the long-term capital stakes of their employees. Some chief executives do emphasize the share-option schemes available for the management elite. They occasionally press their institutional shareholders for more option rights. Sir Ralph Halpern of Burton Group fought a battle with the institutions to allow the directors and senior managers to receive options above the four-times salary limit. It would have been a more admirable campaign if it had been fought in the interests of the many employees instead of the few well-paid managers.

Yet when I lecture to groups of middle managers and employees in other companies and describe to them the NFC values, the interest is never less than intense. I know from their questions that they wish that their own companies could somehow fight the campaign with the external investors to give them similar rights. I believe that the investing institutions would be prepared to listen. After all, we brought a company to the market with our rules of employee-sharing in place. They have not boycotted our shares. On the contrary they have given them the highest rating of any major company in our sector. I believe the institutional investors can be persuaded. What we are short of is companies who want to embrace these values and who are prepared to persuade investors that it is in *their* long-term advantage to grant these concessions.

So much for how employee involvement might spread in industry in general. Of more immediate concern to me is whether the NFC values will survive the short-term shock of the Stock Exchange flotation and the longer-term pressures of the needs to push earnings per share aggressively. In addition, there is taking place a major change in the top management brought about by most of the original buy-out team reaching retirement age at the same time.

210

When the shares were introduced to the Stock Exchange, we gave a straightforward message to the family owners. The future of our unique company now rests with you. If you take up none of the rights and sell your existing shares at more than 10 per cent per annum, there is no way that family control of the business will survive. Each individual had to decide what value he placed on the concept. We had to wait for nearly three months before we could see the result of these individual decisions, and we were not disappointed.

The print-out showed that in the first few months of trading, the family were indeed behaving as long-term investors. There were a little over 38 million new shares issued as a result of the rights offering. Roughly 50 per cent of these were bought by existing family shareholders and 50 per cent were sold on the market. This was a much higher take-up of the rights than we had expected.

Of the shares that were owned by the employees at the time of the introduction, only some 7 per cent were sold. This meant that three months after the introduction the employees actually owned more shares in total than they held before flotation: a much better start than we had hoped for or expected. But although the employees owned more shares, they held a marginally smaller percentage of the total shares in issue because of the extra shares issued to raise the £50m new money. Consequently, the institutional investors had increased their percentage share of the ownership by some 3 per cent.

The table of ownership now looked like this:

	Before flotation per cent of total shares	After flotation per cent of total shares	After flotation per cent of voting rights
Institutions	17	21	16
Employees	31	28	44
Others (including family trusts, pensioners and private investors)	52	51	40

It must be remembered that employee shares command twice the voting power per share of any other shares. So it can be seen that the control of the company still firmly rests in the hands of the employees, their families and the pensioners.

Since May 1989 there has been a marginal drift away from family control. Two forces have been at work in different directions. First of all, the share trust has been buying over £1m of shares every month to satisfy the needs of the two profit-sharing and share-saving schemes. On the other hand, family sales have been moving at a rate marginally in excess of 10 per cent per annum. The employees were standing firm with their sales being at a rate of only 3 per cent per annum, well below the required level.

So far, so good, bearing in mind that there was a pent-up demand for selling. The rate of sales of shares for the six months leading up to flotation was, as would be expected, very much below the average. So there was some catching up to do. But I expect selling to settle down below 10 per cent per annum from now on. The trends so far suggest therefore that the share register will stabilize and will ensure employee and family control into the long-term future.

But the joker in the pack will be the share price. Dealing opened with the early price ranging from 262p to 251p per share. The price has since declined twice to around 230 and twice come back to over 260. We need greater stability than this if our family members are going to feel comfortable about holding in the long term.

We are doing what we can to provide this stability. With the vigorous cash flows coming through from good trading results, we are now buying shares for the profit-sharing scheme instead of issuing new shares, which is how the 1988 profit-sharing needs were substantially met. Buying existing shares instead of issuing new shares helps to sustain demand and harden price. We have continued the policy of giving a best view on the likely profit out-turn for the year. Our trading has been so good that we have been able confidently to forecast an aggressive 30 per cent increase in earnings per share for 1989. Finally, we have promised the shareholders rather more dividends than they were expecting. Income is as important as potential capital gain to many of our investors. It is absolutely vital to the long-term investor.

We are doing other things to try to stimulate demand for the shares. We are seeking to make the profit-sharing scheme punch greater weight than in the past. This can be done in two ways. Firstly, by improving the incentives which encourage people to save for shares. The present scheme is that for each three shares an individual buys, he receives one share as a bonus. About 50 per cent of employees are involved in this scheme – but we must find ways of increasing the number. For example, we could offer two bonus shares for every three bought, thus giving more incentive to individuals to save. Secondly, we are seeing if we can make use of the new Finance Act's assistance to ESOPs (employee stock ownership plans). We believe that by diverting, say, £2m each year out of the profit-sharing kitty into a separate trust and then using this as collateral, we should be able to borrow an extra £2.5m from the banks. This makes £2m into £4.5m which the trust will then be able to use to buy this value of shares. The shares will be held for future distribution to the employees.

By 1990 we expect the profit-sharing allocation to employees to be £20m. By refocusing our scheme in the way I have described, the £20m could be made to purchase some £28m of shares per annum.

The continuing challenge will be to make the profit-sharing schemes more and more inventive and effective, to enable shares to be recycled into employee ownership rather than being sold to the institutions.

But there will be forces at play which could tempt future management to turn away from putting employee/family control at the top of the strategic agenda. As I have said, our employee focus means that it is difficult, if not impossible, to use the full range of corporate weaponry that is available to the normal company for expansion or for increasing earnings per share.

For example, NFC do not have the option of selling off a company with a significant number of employees, unless these employees agree that they want to leave the NFC group. It is simply not credible for the directors to say on the one hand that they value their employees and want their deeper financial commitment to the business, and on the other to sell them out of NFC against their wishes. If we have parts of the business which strategically do not fit, we either have to persuade the employees working in those businesses that they would be better off under different ownership, or live with the misfit. It is a difficult task to persuade employees that their best interests lie elsewhere. Now NFC policy is clear, companies leave NFC only if the employees working in them vote to leave. We have had two examples where small businesses employing not many people have been sold, but in both cases they were sold to employee buy-outs.

Future managements may be tempted, particularly if trading in the core business is less buoyant, to rid themselves of this restriction. After all, the argument will go, it does not destroy our people focus for the employees that remain, and those that are going will be in a better home. These are siren voices. Employees are not stupid. Management cannot be prepared, for whatever reason, to sell a business despite the wishes of the employees, while at the same time convince the remaining employees that their caring, people-focused policy is anything other than expedient cant.

Another siren which might seduce NFC's employee values on to the rocks is the City adviser with his bag of takeover temptations. NFC today has a high reputation and a high stock market valuation. Without diluting our earnings per share we could take over one or other of our major competitors. The purchase price would be too high for us to use only cash, as the mountain of debt would make our new healthy balance sheet look very sick. There are better ways available, as our advisers will feel it is their duty to signal. Part, if not all, of the purchase price could be offered in NFC shares. Indeed the investors in the company we are being invited to attack would prefer shares. In this way they do not realize a capital gain. *But*, every issue of shares of this kind will weaken employee control because the percentage of the company owned by the family will be diluted. The arguments in purely financial terms will be compelling. The market expects a company with NFC's high rating to be aggressive. Indeed, there is no good financial reason why it should not take over badly-performing competitors, particularly if it can do so at a price which on its present profit performance will enhance its earnings per share. It seems pretty feeble to be saying, 'It is against the core of our mission statement to go down this apparent primrose path . . . It is also against our values to take over workforces that really don't want to join us.' All we can point out is that the size of the business grew three times in seven years without one contested takeover or by issuing any new equity. But as the memory dims and new young management comes to the top, the short cut to achieve aggressive growth by major competitor takeovers using equity will seem attractive. Corporate values, it will be argued, must be flexible and change with the times.

Another temptation to change the focus of the mission statement lies in the very success that has been achieved. It will become easy for a management that has known only success to begin to attribute that success solely to the brilliance of the strategies and their own management flair. It is hard to prove that employees equally contribute by wanting and welcoming change. They welcome change because they feel that they in part own the strategy and that they will share fully in its success. Participative management is often tiresome; it takes endless debate and discussion. It holds back instant decision-taking. The temptation will be to continue with the profit-sharing and the employee share ownership programmes, but quietly to forget the involvement and participative side of the equation. Let us rely solely on the motivation of greed in the individual and forget that he also needs vision.

NFC faces this temptation every day of every week, in every one of the companies. The leadership of the business must and does fight for the vision. If the leadership decided that the vision cake was no longer worth the ha'pence, it would not be long before NFC reverted in style and performance to that of any other business. The temptations are great but the reward for their resistance has been shown to be greater, both in performance and in the job satisfaction of the people who work in the NFC.

It takes a long time to change the culture of a business. For example, to turn a company that is production driven to one that is customer driven. It takes stamina, as there is always a natural tendency in people to run back downhill to that which they know, and feel comfortable with. It is an even longer haul to establish new values in an enterprise. Values are the instincts which run the business. They are deep-seated and are not constantly debated. The kind of values that a business may choose from include integrity, fair trading, value for money, cheapest, high quality regardless of price, employee focus, sharing, customer first and last, racy, 'must win at all costs', ruthless – the list is almost endless. Whichever are selected, they become the accepted norm and standards of behaviour that are as natural to a business as a young child pulling her hand from a fire. When two businesses where values are different come together, problems arise unless the values are reconciled. What happened with the Blue Arrow affair resulted from a different set of values within the same bank, National Westminster. The values of the high street bank – honesty, conservatism, and avoidance of risk – clearly sit unhappily alongside the values of a merchant bank that has to be aggressive, innovative and judged only by its ability to win. Whether these two sets of values can ever sit happily alongside each other is questionable. The damage of the merchant banking revelations to the clearing bank was enormous, not only in commercial terms. As one NatWest high street banker said to me, 'I never in my wildest dreams believed I would have to apologize for, or be required to justify, my bank's business ethics.' If values are confused, danger lurks.

On the other hand, particular corporate values attract different types of people. The Marks & Spencer values built up over a hundred years attract a different type of employee to the 'pile them high, sell them cheap' policy which used to be the Tesco mission. It is interesting to see how, under the inspired leadership of Sir Ian MacLaurin, Tesco has changed its values and its market stance with it. It has moved up market. The value change has also brought measurable improvements in the quality of the employees and the suppliers who work with and for the business.

NFC needs more time for its values to take root. It needs at least another generation of top management who believe in these values and can promote them without constantly challenging, debating and pulling them up by the roots to see if they are growing.

There will be pressure on the new team, but I do believe that they will protect and promote the NFC values of employee involvement, high service levels to our customers, and sharing the success. After all, each of them knew and worked with NFC when its values were different. They have seen the success and satisfaction enjoyed by NFC and its employees since their adoption. They have seen the approval that the outside world has given to the new values. They will not lightly abandon them.

As for me, I am slowly withdrawing from the business. Within eighteen months I will have retired and be enjoying a new life with my new wife Lydia and our baby daughter Emma. As I write, another baby is on the way. We are surrounded by horses, sheep, ponies, cats, dogs and rabbits. My three elder children, Gail, Michael and Mandy, are all leading full lives, enjoying business success, and yet we manage to be a close and united family. There is no conflict between the older family and the new. I am a happy, fortunate man. My new life will be a life away from the day-to-day pressure of accountability for the profit, share price and employment hopes of thousands of people. But NFC will be in good hands, as I know those who will be leading it share the business and human values that they themselves have helped to create.

It will survive.

Index

223